Asher

A JOURNEY OF SURVIVAL
A Young Boy's Odyssey from Hungary
through Auschwitz and Jaworznow, to Eretz Yisrael

Asher Bar-Nir

A JOURNEY OF SURVIVAL

A Young Boy's Odyssey from Hungary
through Auschwitz and Jaworznow to Eretz Yisrael

Yad Vashem ★ Jerusalem
The International Institute for Holocaust Research

Asher Bar-Nir
A Journey of Survival

Language Editor: Art Braunstein
Production Editor: Gayle Green

ISBN 978-965-308-386-8

Typesetting: Judith Sternberg
Produced by: Art Plus, Jerusalem

Printed in Israel

To the memory of my parents,
Ilona and Zoltán Sichermann,
my Uncle Zsigmond (Öcsi) Bleier
and my best friend, Pista Klein.

CONTENTS

INTRODUCTION

It was Sunday, March 19, 1944.

I was thirteen and a half years old.

The German Army had just marched into Hungary and put an end to the relative independence enjoyed by this small country, which actively fought with the Germans against the Soviet Union and, even up to that stage in the Second World War, was one of the most loyal allies of the Nazi regime.

Hungary's Prime Minister, Miklos Kallay, although not a very bright individual, understood like anyone who had even a little brainpower, a little *sechel,* that Germany was losing the war and it was only a question of time and more destruction, misery and death before the Nazi regime finally collapsed. Kallay tried to juggle between the Allies and the Germans. People were whispering about secret negotiations underway between Great Britain and Hungary for British paratroopers to occupy Hungary with the cooperation of the Kallay government. I don't know how true those rumors were. In any case, the Germans prevented the secret negotiations between the Allies and Hungary from bearing any fruit.

In mid-March 1944, Hitler summoned Admiral Miklos Horthy, the Hungarian Head of State, to his headquarters in Klessheim and reprimanded him on account of the "treachery" of the Kallay Government and informed Horthy that Hungary would be occupied by German troops.

So, on that fateful Sunday morning in March 1944, German troops marched into Hungary, meeting no resistance from the Hungarian Army. I didn't realize then that the first phase of my life had just ended. The phase of a happy and pampered child, loved by his parents and treated by them as the center of the universe, had terminated.

On that morning, I was still in bed. It was Sunday and of course there was no school. There must have been some noise, which roused me because I was suddenly wide awake and noticed my father standing before the large sofa, which served as my bed. For some reason or other my mother was also in the room when my father, obviously very excited, started to speak. He had come from his office, despite the fact that it was a Sunday when people were supposed to rest. However, my father, who was most devoted to his duties, often went to work on Sundays.

CHAPTER 1

LIFE BEFORE THE WAR

MY TOWN

We lived in Nyiregyháza, a small town of 50,000 inhabitants at the time, of which approximately fifteen percent were Jewish. Most of the population in Hungary was Catholic and the rest either Evangelic, as the followers of Luther were named, or Reform, as the followers of Calvin were called.

Nyiregyháza is located 245 kilometers east of Budapest, the capital, and some 150 kilometers west of the pre-war Soviet border. We had an electric tram service in the town with the last station adjacent to my father's place of work. There, at the terminus, the tram conductor just removed the lever by which he controlled the vehicle's motion and passed to the reverse side of the tram. He would place the control lever there and the tram was all set to travel in the opposite direction.

One pair of rails served both directions, running to and from the market place in the city's center. Exactly halfway between both terminuses there was a parallel extra pair of rails some eleven meters long, to allow a tram coming from the opposite direction to safely pass. During the summer months, this narrow-rail tram also served Sóstó, which was our vacation resort. Sóstó was approximately five or six kilometers away from the market place in the midst of a beautiful but not too large forest.

Most of the gentile population of Nyiregyháza was antisemitic—the hostile atmosphere against us could not have been misread. Antisemitism was in the air; one could breathe the antagonism against the Jews. Still, I personally, perhaps foolishly, although often chased by youngsters shouting antisemitic slogans, felt safe in Nyiregyháza and freely moved around the town by foot, by tram or riding my bicycle.

In the summer of 1987, I revisited Nyiregyháza with my wife Tova and my youngest daughter, Merav. I, who by then was an "outsider", a "foreigner", in Nyiregyháza, wanted to observe the population. Many of the inhabitants looked obviously to be descendants of gypsies or were gypsies themselves. Not that a gypsy is in any way more antisemitic than a Hungarian, maybe it is the other way around. I looked at these people and thought that they were complete strangers to me.

In New York, London or even Paris, I don't usually feel that I am among total strangers. At this time, however, I felt Nyiregyháza to be much more "alien" than any of those cities. The whole town was perplexing. I was among strangers. I didn't see any familiar faces. I must have been longing for the Jewish faces long since gone, most of them murdered by the Germans years before in 1944 and 1945, and the others, like I, who had emigrated. Not seeing any of them I found myself in a strangely quaint land. I wondered and asked myself, having grown up here in Nyiregyháza, how did I then, as a child, feel safe and at home in this place where all these strangers didn't even attempt to hide their hostility. Not to mention the fact that Auschwitz, with its gas chambers, was only a couple of hundred kilometers away. Luckily, when I was a child, I didn't know about this geographical fact nor did I know, of course, what Auschwitz was all about.

How naive we all, or more accurately, most of us were during the war. We actually thought that Nyiregyháza and Hungary were our home. We wanted to believe that this was our homeland. It was such a tragic mistake, this delusion, and we paid dearly for it.

MY HOME

Back in 1944, we were living in a house that was owned by Futura (I suppose the name is somehow related to the English word "future"), the firm my father had been working for since graduating from Kereskedelmi High School. Futura was partially, or possibly, fully owned by the Italian insurance conglomerate Generali. Futura was mainly in the grain storage business but it also had facilities for manufacturing sunflower oil and distilling alcohol.

We lived just across from the railroad station and only a four to five minute walk to my father's office. This office was located in one of several big grain warehouses and was alongside the railroad to accommodate the wagons carrying grain. The tracks of the tram service I mentioned were only some five meters away from the western side of our property and, therefore, I usually heard the jingle of the trams passing by.

Our house was big, with a huge orchard and a good-sized flower garden. The entire property occupied over 5,000 square meters. The house itself was some 200 square meters. A little gate, located diagonally across from the railroad station, on the west side of the property, served as the main entrance to the courtyard. The house itself was located approximately five meters from our property's fence. The flower garden was on the opposite side of the house and the orchard on its south.

There also was a small seven to ten meter wide yard hedged between the northern fence and the house, which served as a small chicken farm. The income generated from selling the eggs served as my mother's "private" fund. It was her "egg money", as we called it in the family.

A small well provided water for the house. Pipes led water that was manually pumped from this well to a small tank located at the house. Thus, we had running water in the bathroom and the kitchen. A big, mentally disabled young man came to our home once or twice a month to pump water from the well to the house.

A corridor ran along the whole length of the house with an entrance at each end. It had three equally-sized living rooms as well as a hall, pantry, kitchen and bathroom. Of the three rooms, the one on the south side was my parents' bedroom; another on the north side was mine, which also served as the family dining room. The living room in between was the salon, but very seldom used. Our big piano, which had belonged to my mother's family before my parents married, and formed part of her dowry, was usually located in my room. However, from time to time, it was moved back and forth between my room and the salon, whenever my mother wanted to experiment with the layout.

◆

"The Germans are occupying Hungary," my father announced. "I have spoken on the phone with Mr. Gábor and he told me that German troops entered Budapest this morning."

Mr. Gábor was my father's "legendary" boss, whose name I often heard mentioned in our home. Gábor was born Jewish, but later in life converted to Catholicism. I should emphasize that despite the assimilation among most of Hungary's Jewish population only a small minority discarded the Jewish religion and became Christian.

Mr. Gábor was part of that minority. He thought highly of my father and was very fond of him. I never saw him in person of course because his office was in Budapest, and I doubt that my mother ever met him either. However, since this terrible information came directly from *him*, we had no doubt in our minds that it was a true and reliable piece of news.

It turned out that Gábor had called my father on the telephone, which was remarkable in itself in those days when telephones in Hungary were scarce and long-distance calls were rare, to inform him about this ominous turn of events. A phone call from Budapest to our town of Nyiregyháza in those days underlined the dramatic significance of the news.

I believe that all three of us—my mother, my father and even myself—understood right away the significance of what was taking place and maybe also realized that from now on nothing was going to be the same.

In a second, our lives had been fatefully altered. I was less than fourteen years old, but quite knowledgeable about developments in the war. I had overheard conversations among my parents and their friends and also secretly listened to the BBC many times together with my parents. The BBC was the best source of reliable information. It gave hope to all who aspired to the defeat of Nazism and the victory of the Allies.

MY FAMILY

My father, Zoltán Sichermann, was born in Nyiregyháza, as was I. This town, both before and after the Great or First World War, was part of Hungary. My mother was born Ilona Bleier in Besztercebánya. At the time, both towns were part of the Austro-Hungarian Empire. Her town was renamed after the Great War as Banská Bystrica when it became part of the newly created Czechoslovak State. She was born on April 7, 1909, so that on the day the Germans marched into Hungary my mother was just about thirty-five years old. My father was born in 1900, and was to become forty-four years old on August 30, 1944.

I realize now how young my parents were then because as I write this book, my youngest daughter Merav, born on June 6, 1965, is in her mid-forties, several years older than my mother was on that fateful day. My older daughter Michal, born on October 25, 1957, is over fifty, far older than my father was on March 19, 1944.

Asher's parents, Zoltán and Ilona,
at their engagement

♦

My parents met under very romantic circumstances. Father and mother became acquainted in a fencing club. He was less than twenty nine years old and she was nineteen. I think that maybe only Jews were members of that particular club. The Jews had a very active cultural and sporting life in Nyiregyháza. The *Koer*, or Circle, was the Jews' only cultural center, not that gentiles were forbidden to join, but none of them did.

There were also two sport clubs in Nyiregyháza, Nyetve and Nyekise. One of them was more attended by Jews than gentiles, and the other just the opposite. However, I have forgotten which was which. Anyhow, as young adults, both my mother and father fenced. I remember that we even had some medals at home, earned by my father during his fencing career. They came to know each other at the club. My father left a note in my mother's fencing gloves. The note started with something like, "Dear unknown, I very much would like to meet you... ."

And thus they started dating. I don't have much information about their courtship, but it must have been quite short because they married in 1929. My mother was twenty years old and my father twenty-nine. Nine years of difference in age between husband and wife was quite normal at the time.

To be completely honest, I have to admit that I really don't know too much about my parents. What sort of people were they *really*? What was the *true nature* of their relationship as a couple? I only knew them as my parents, with the emphasis on "my", i.e., the way they related to me. I was under the impression that I was the center of their lives. Neither did I bother, nor did I know much, about their preoccupation with all the other aspects of life.

Of course, during the war, everyone in Hungary was busy following the events of the various battles and fronts and speculating when and how it would all end and what would become of us. But even then, unless war forcefully disrupts one's normal existence, people live with their day-to-day worries, likes and dislikes, ambitions, prejudices, etc. They experience all the events and emotions that make up life.

As far as my parents are concerned, I don't know much about their anxieties. After all, I was only just over thirteen years old when everything in our lives was about to change drastically. Still, I would very much like to believe that my parents loved each other and had a harmonious life together.

Nevertheless, I recollect one chain of events based on my mother's jealousy. I think, however, that objectively my father had more reason to be envious than the other way around. The incident is very vivid in my memory and it took place during the summer of 1943. My mother was suspicious of the exceptionally good relationship she thought my father had with a gentile female colleague of his who worked "uptown", not in the same office even as my father. I think this woman was unmarried. My mother became jealous and decided to have my father taste the same medicine, and make him suspect that she also had somebody courting her.

So my mother somehow let him know that she was going to be in Sóstó on this or that day, at such and such a time, accompanied by her "suitor". My

Asher and his parents

father promptly showed up at the time indicated by my mother's provocation and saw my mother and her "suitor".

One should try to understand the significance of my father being absent from work on a normal weekday if even for a few hours. It must have been very important for him to find out who this mysterious suitor might be. So, who was her mysterious beau? You guessed right, it was I, their son!

My father saw my mother and me together and realized that she had made fun of him. I suppose he was both angry and relieved at the same time. I wasn't surprised at all that during the one-hour tram journey back home my parents didn't exchange even a single word between them. Looking back on this episode, now with the "wisdom" of my many years, I can't resist smiling. After all, they were still "children" then, jealous and, most probably and hopefully, loving children.

The ever-evolving relationship between parents and children is very intriguing. First, when a baby is born it is fully dependent on his or her parents, mainly the mother. With the years, this dependence is gradually reduced and later in life it begins to turn in the other direction. Parents become more and more dependent on their children. Then, in the end, and providing a parent reaches a ripe old age, there is a complete reversal in the relationship. The parent becomes fully dependent on his or her offspring. In my case, because of the tragedy of the Holocaust, I never came even close to experiencing all the phases of this saga because I lost my parents when I was still a child and they were still so very young.

However, now as a father, I am in the midst of the later stages of this evolution as far as my relationships with my daughters go and have personal experience, for the first time, of the changing relationship between parents and children.

♦

As I said, I think that my father had an objective reason to be envious of my mother, more than the other way around. My mother was a very attractive woman and most probably was aware of this fact. Men liked her company and flocked around her like butterflies attracted to a flower.

One incident sticks in my mind. It happened during late 1943 or early 1944, of course before the Germans occupied Hungary. In those days, I would travel all alone once a week by train for my piano lessons in Debrecen, a larger town, fifty kilometers south of Nyiregyháza. I will discuss these piano lessons later in more detail.

It was an hour-long journey in each direction. One afternoon after the lesson with Miss Margit Höchtel, I walked, as always, to the railroad station in Debrecen to catch my train back to Nyiregyháza. For some reason, I made an error and instead of boarding the train to Nyiregyháza in the north, I found myself on a different train, which was traveling to the east. I immediately noticed my mistake once the train started to move. However, I had to wait for the train to stop at the next station in order to get off. It seemed like an eternity before the train finally halted. I disembarked and found myself in a village the name of which I have forgotten. I started to walk and somehow located a grocery store approximately one kilometer from the railroad station. The owner of the store was Jewish and luckily had a telephone in his shop. He allowed me to use it and I called my father. We didn't have a telephone at home but my father had one in his office.

My father spoke with this kind Jewish man in the store and he gave me money for the train ticket back to Debrecen and then to Nyiregyháza. So, late in the afternoon, I arrived at the station in Nyiregyháza. On the platform waiting for me were my father, my mother and, to my great surprise, also Mr. Luka Jenő Imecsfalvy, the Principal of Polgári High School. At this time, I no longer attended his school because during the previous summer I had switched to the Gymnasium, which was the more prestigious high school.

So what was he doing there at the station, waiting for me together with my parents? Imecsfalvy, in his late forties, was a good-looking man. I remember once seeing his wife who looked like she was his mother, an "old" and unattractive lady. His presence there at the railroad station puzzled me then and it still puzzles me today. What was he doing there?

My parents were of course happy to see me safe and sound after my adventure, but I saw that Imecsfalvy felt out of place. No wonder. He had no business being there. I can think of only one logical explanation. As I just related, I had called my father by phone from that village where I accidentally found myself. My father couldn't have alerted my mother by phone because we had none at home. Therefore, he most probably went home to fetch her so that they could go together to the railroad station. Mr. Imecsfalvy most probably was at our house at the time and had no choice but to join my parents to greet the lost son.

What was Imecsfalvy doing in our house that afternoon? There certainly existed some potential mischief in that situation. On the other hand, there couldn't have been any pre-planned misconduct involving my mother because she must have known that I would have met Imecsfalvy in our house had I arrived at the correct time. In addition, I don't remember seeing my father angry or my mother embarrassed, but I recall observing Imecsfalvy feeling out of place, which he most certainly was. Therefore, most probably, all this was just an innocent incident with a logical explanation. I, however, still keep thinking about it.

THE GERMAN OCCUPATION

But let's return to that ominous, terrible day of March 19, 1944.

The shock of learning that the Germans were marching into Hungary was magnified by waking up from the illusion we had been living in. First, we believed that because Hungary was such a close ally of Germany, the Germans would not occupy the country. In addition, late 1943 and early 1944 looked like a brighter period for the Jews in Hungary. That's what we, at least, wanted to believe.

The Red Army was advancing from the east and was already approaching the Hungarian border of the Carpathian Mountains. Prime Minister Miklos Kallay was secretly negotiating with the Allies. Some anti-Jewish regulations had been mollified, although only de facto. We were hoping that the war would be over in a jiffy. And now suddenly everything changed.

Mother Nature does not always cooperate with the calamities conceived by the human beast, and this late winter Sunday turned out to be a beautiful sunny day. My father went to work on that Sunday and I got out of bed.

Our live-in maid, Margot, was still at home and was preparing herself for her Sunday off. Margot was probably no more than eighteen years old at the time. She was a simple village girl, doing daily chores for us while my mother ran the house and directed Margot's activities. She was a pretty girl with red cheeks and a healthy composure. She had come to work for us a couple of years before, directly from her village.

Margot was happy to get away from home and the tyranny of her drunkard father. My mother taught her to cook, to dress and how to carry herself. Margot seemed to be very appreciative of her stay with us and proud of her position. She was told the news about the Germans, but I am not sure that she comprehended all its potential consequences. Margot seemed to be very loyal to our family in the days that followed the German march into Hungary. She later even declared her wish to wear the yellow star, as we were forced to do, and even wanted to voluntarily join us in the ghetto. Of course her gesture wasn't very realistic and I am not sure that Margot really meant it.

When I returned to Nyiregyháza in the spring of 1945, I saw her by chance on Bethlehem Street. I was astonished to observe that Margot had under her armpit my mother's blue imitation crocodile skin handbag. For some reason, I never even stopped to talk to her and although it was clear that she recognized me, she didn't address me either. Maybe we were both just embarrassed. Therefore, I never found out whether she participated in the looting of our home, which took place after we were deported, or whether my mother gave her the handbag as a parting gift.

◆

I imagine that some people at the time did understand the possible and potential consequences of the German occupation. However, even the Jews didn't fully comprehend, or maybe didn't want to face up to all the details of the terrible fate the Nazis were preparing for us. The most realistic about the fate of the Jews in Hungary, even before the German occupation, were the Zionists. It so happened that for the afternoon of March 19, 1944, a meeting of the *Hashomer Hatzair* youth movement was planned in one of the Jewish elementary school's halls. Because of the developments of that day, the meeting was cancelled.

It should be emphasized that only a small minority of Hungarian Jews were Zionists. One could classify the majority of the Jews, most of them non-Zionists, as belonging to one of two groups. There were the very religious who voluntarily segregated themselves from Hungarian gentile society and preferred to exist in their own mental ghetto. Then, there were those others, belonging to the larger group of the two, who strove for full assimilation into Hungarian society and culture. The very religious spoke Yiddish among themselves and knew very little Hungarian. Members of the second group only spoke Hungarian and had an aversion to Yiddish.

I joined the Zionists of *Hashomer Hatzair*, approximately a year or a year and a half before the German occupation. It was the leading Zionist movement in Nyiregyháza at the time. I joined the Movement at the urging of my schoolmates Pista Klein, who was my best friend, and Pista Lipkovits who, besides being my friend, was also my cousin. Most probably we were and are third cousins because although my father and Pista's mother were cousins they couldn't have been first cousins since their parents weren't brother or sister.

At the time, I was, like most of the youngsters, under the strong influence of our revered Rabbi and teacher, Dr. Aladár Wax. Dr. Wax was an ardent Zionist, a charismatic figure, adored by myself and by many Jewish students in Nyiregyháza. Even today, when I am typing his name, I am filled with emotion. When I first met Dr. Wax, I was a student in the Polgari first grade. Polgari was a less prestigious school than the Gymnasium, which I later transferred to with Pista Klein in September 1943, before entering eighth grade.

From Polgari, one could advance after four years of study only to the Kereskedelmi, for an additional four years. The Kereskedelmi was a commercial high school. Graduates would become bookkeepers and the like. Keep in mind, however, that bookkeepers in Hungary were highly appreciated and enjoyed similar prestige in society to that of CPAs today in the US. On the other hand, if one graduated from a gymnasium one could enter any university to become a medical doctor, a lawyer, a graduate engineer, etc.

Because of the anti-Jewish regulations, I couldn't go to the Gymnasium after finishing the fourth grade of the Jewish elementary school. Therefore, I had to go to Polgari. In order to toughen the choice for Jewish students who wished to attend the Gymnasium the fees for us were set exceptionally high. As I recall, the yearly fee in the Gymnasium for a Jewish student was 600 pengő. Two hundred had to be paid at registration and then an additional forty pengő each month for the eleven months of the school year. It was a lot of money. My father earned 300–400 pengő a month, which was considered a nice salary. Gentile students had to pay only a fraction of what was demanded of the Jews.

I should also mention that, according to the recollection of Robi Vermes, an additional reason behind the fact that only one Jewish boy, Andris Citrom, from our class went to the Gymnasium after elementary school was because our Chief Rabbi in Nyiregyháza, Dr. Bernstein, forbade Jewish boys to go to the Gymnasium because of this discrimination.

As already mentioned, however, the political climate in Hungary in 1943 was becoming less discriminatory and so it came about that my friend Pista Klein and I were able to apply to the Gymnasium. Most of our 1943 summer vacation was spent studying for the special admission test, Latin and various other subjects, which were not taught at Polgari.

Anyhow, I first met Dr. Wax when I was still in Polgari High School. One day we were informed that he was to be our new religion teacher. Dr. Wax had previously taught religion in the Gymnasium, but was removed at the request of some of the more influential parents. Why was he kicked out? The reason was that Dr. Wax was an ardent Zionist who wasn't shy about his views, just the opposite. Those among the "better" Jews who were for total assimilation and whose sons attended the Gymnasium and not Polgari didn't want their youngsters exposed to the "dangerous" Zionist ideas of Dr. Wax and therefore arranged for him to be transferred from his teaching job in the Gymnasium to Polgari. I don't know where Dr. Bernstein, our Chief Rabbi, stood on this issue. A junior rabbi by the name of Dr. Károly Jolesz was brought to Nyiregyháza to take over Dr. Wax's responsibilities in the Gymnasium. Dr. Jolesz, unlike Dr. Wax, survived the Holocaust and after the war settled in Israel. For many years after that he served as Rabbi to some of the Jewish communities in Latin America.

Dr. Wax was charismatic, good-looking, sarcastic and a little arrogant and we, his students, admired him. I remember my shock when he told us in class, during one of the lectures, "You should always keep in mind that you are a Jew first and a Hungarian only after that." "What is this man blabbering about?" I said to myself! "I am a Hungarian whose religion is Jewish and not a Jew who happens to live in Hungary, as Dr. Wax is hinting." Slowly pondering the meaning of what Dr. Wax was trying to impress upon us, and assisted by my friends Pista Klein and Pista Lipkovits, whose older brothers were also Zionists, I came to realize that Dr. Wax was right. I am a Jew. I belong to the Jewish people. I happened to have Hungarian citizenship only because I was born in Hungary.

Dr. Wax was not only a charismatic figure but a gifted orator as well. When the congregation got advance notice that he was about to address the Status Quo Ante Congregation, (similar to a Conservative congregation in the

U.S. today) the synagogue was full to capacity. Many in the audience were loudly crying while they listened to his speech.

Dr. Wax was married to my first grade elementary school teacher, Aunt Erzsike, as we called her. Their first and only baby girl was taught to speak Hebrew before she spoke Hungarian. This was an unusual feat in Hungary, to say the least. Although Dr. Wax was a religious man, he was also active within the "atheist" *Hashomer Hatzair*, which was the leading Zionist movement in Nyiregyháza and possibly in Hungary as well.

I found out more only recently when I accidentally met someone who was one of the activists in *Hashomer Hatzair* in Hungary. This person, in the spring of 1944, especially traveled by train to Nyiregyháza from Budapest (thus endangering himself) with false papers for Dr. Wax, his wife and child, when we were all already in the ghetto. He tried to persuade Dr. Wax to escape from the ghetto to Budapest. Dr. Wax refused. He said that his place was with his community in those days of tragedy and wouldn't leave the ghetto. As it turned out, it was a proud, honest but foolish decision. There wasn't much he could do to help us. Had he gone to Budapest he might have, at least, saved his family and himself.

Dr. Wax and his family stayed in Nyiregyháza and shared the fate of us all. I heard that he was beaten to death in one concentration camp while his wife and daughter perished in Birkenau, most probably on the very day of their arrival. I saw Dr. Wax alive for the last time in Auschwitz, but I will recount this episode later in my story.

♦

Anyhow, on that fateful day of March 19, 1944, we were supposed to have a Zionist meeting but I was told by my *madrich* (the leader of my group), called Asher, (my Hebrew name is also Asher) that the meeting had been postponed.

Asher was eighteen or nineteen years old at the time. His parents' house was just behind ours. He had some lameness in one arm, which might have been the reason why he wasn't called up for *Munkaszolgálat*, the forced labor service for Jews within the military that was introduced during the war. While doing *Munkaszolgálat* in the Ukraine, thousands of Hungarian Jews met their death, many at the hands of the Hungarian soldiers, the so-called *Keret*, or overseers, who guarded them. The harsh, cold winter weather and other perils of the war also took their toll on these unfortunate human beings.

But let's return to Zionism. I have to confess my gullibility because at that time in my life everyone who was a Zionist or some way connected to the Movement, in my view, was just perfect. As far as I was concerned, such a person was most probably an "idealist". This was my point of view regarding Asher as well. I respected him very much and most certainly he was a very serious, reliable and devoted person.

♦

A day or two after the German occupation, a new government was nominated by Miklós Horthy, the *Kormányzó* or Regent of Hungary. Horthy had taken power after the First World War in 1919 and was the "pioneer" in Europe in introducing anti-Jewish laws, regulations and antisemitism in general. As time passed, he "softened" towards the Jews, or so the Jews in Hungary tried to make themselves believe. People were saying, "Whatever was happening to the Jews in the rest of Europe couldn't happen here in Hungary because Horthy will never allow anyone, even the Germans, to harm us." How wrong they were.

Jews were also whispering among themselves that Horthy's wife regularly played cards with the richest of the rich Jewish "nobility" in the Royal Castle of Buda, Horthy's official residence. Very discrete rumors were also circulating about "some Jewish blood in the family of Horthy's wife". One of her grandmothers or a great-grandmother was supposed to have been Jewish. "Oh, my God, how wonderful if only it were even partially true."

Despite this, the news network announced after March 19, 1944 that Horthy had nominated a far right-wing and extremely antisemitic government with Döme Sztójay, the former Hungarian Ambassador to Germany, as Prime Minister.

The most urgent task of the new government, right after its nomination, was to make the already existing laws against the Jews much harsher and completely intolerable. Among other measures, as of April 5, 1944, every Jew was to affix a yellow star of a certain size to his clothing and was threatened to be severely punished should he/she be seen outside without it.

I even remember that the instructions regarding the sewing of the yellow star on the clothing were so precise as to prescribe that "the stitches were to be close to each other in such a manner that a pencil couldn't be inserted between them".

My father was given notice and fired from his job, but being the diligent person he was, continued to go regularly to his former workplace to ensure that his colleague and, now successor, Mr. Buji, would have a smooth transition to his new responsibilities. I have to admit that the Buji family was one of the few Christian Hungarians with whom my parents had social contact. The Bujis had two children, Feri, a boy of my age, and a younger daughter, Marika, I believe.

MY LIFE IN 1944 HUNGARY

Before I go on, I would like to describe myself as I was then, my family, our background.

As I have mentioned, I was thirteen and a half years old. I was a pampered child who was led to believe by his parents that the whole world revolved around him. I was an only child. An only child potentially has a much higher chance of being pampered and even spoilt than a child who has brothers and/or sisters. From correspondence between my mother and my Aunt Edit who lived in Budapest, I later, much later, found out that my parents decided that their financial situation didn't permit them to properly raise more than one child.

It was very important for my parents to provide me with the best possible education. Therefore, even before I was elementary school age, and only five years old, they hired an Austrian *Fraulein* to converse in German with me. I remember the long walks I had to take with her speaking German.

Then, when I was enrolled in second grade, I started to learn to play the piano and one year later I commenced the study of English. I studied piano with a Mrs. Führer, a Jewish lady whose husband was an engineer who owned a store in the most prestigious area of Nyiregyháza, selling electrical equipment and appliances such as existed in Hungary in the 1930s.

Mrs. Führer was a lean, thin, tall lady in her thirties without any children. The rumor was that she had had surgery that prevented her from bearing children. In the summer of 1943, Mrs. Führer held a concert performed by her students, on which occasion I played the piano. Then and there, the general opinion was that I was quite gifted for the piano. My parents then sought the advice of Mrs. Stark who was considered an authority on music, and it was decided that I should advance to a better piano teacher.

The Stark family was rich and belonged to elite Jewish society in Nyiregyháza. They had a daughter called Marika, with rusty hair and freckles. Marika was my age, but I don't recall us ever speaking to each other. After returning from the concentration camp in 1945, I found out that Mr. Stark, the head of the family, was a Communist and had been arrested and jailed under the Horthy regime.

Anyhow, following my "examination" by Mrs. Stark, my mother took me to the much larger town of Debrecen, which was actually second only to Budapest. I was introduced to Margit Höchtel, and had to play the piano for her so she could judge my talent and level of performance. She agreed to take me on as her private student. Miss Höchtel, in her early fifties at the time, was quite a well-known pianist, often heard on the radio, and a teacher at the Academy of Music in Debrecen as well. I listened to her radio broadcasts on several occasions.

Miss Höchtel used to be my mother's piano teacher before she married. Apparently my grandmother had similar ambitions regarding my mother as my mother had for me.

I had weekly lessons in Miss Höchtel's apartment, located adjacent to the Academy of Music in Debrecen. She was a very plain woman, a spinster of German origin who lived with her mother, an elderly lady in her seventies. She had very soft fingers, cut her fingernails very short and used no nail polish at all. This fact was in contrast to the long stiff fingers with red fingernails of Mrs. Führer, indicating very clearly to me that Miss Höchtel was the more serious pianist of the two.

There was a life-size picture of Hitler just behind the piano, so all the time that I played in her studio I had to look at this monster. I thought at the time, and I still believe, that being a spinster and a German, Miss Höchtel most probably had a "crush" on Hitler. Anyhow, during the autumn and winter of 1943–44, I took the train once a week to travel the fifty kilometers from Nyiregyháza to Debrecen and back for my piano lessons.

After March 19, 1944, my parents hypothesized about asking Miss Höchtel to hide me. But this plan was left with no actual action taken beyond the stage of bold speculation. My parents didn't raise such a possibility with her and so we never found out what her reaction would have been.

After I returned from the concentration camp in 1945, and knew that I would go to live with my Aunt Edit in Budapest, I went to visit Miss Höchtel and her mother in Debrecen. I had nothing vicious on my mind by this visit, I was too naive at the time for nasty intentions. I came only to see how they were doing, and ask for a letter of introduction to the Music Academy in Budapest. After all, they hadn't done anything wrong as far as I was concerned. However, now that the war was nearing its end and the Red Army was occupying Hungary, the Höchtels panicked upon seeing me.

I suppose they were afraid because of the life-size Hitler portrait that they knew I had seen so many times before, hanging proudly behind the piano. Needless to say that in 1945, after the war, the portrait was gone and there wasn't a trace or even discoloration on the wall which would have indicated that a large picture used to hang there, testifying to the strong Nazi sympathies of mother and daughter. They were relieved to learn that I had only come for a letter and gave it to me.

◆

I had a number of English teachers, one after the other, who gave me private lessons. The woman who was my last tutor in English and taught me for the longest time was Miss Kató Klein. She was a spinster in her thirties, an unattractive woman who had a very repulsive smell.

Miss Klein had left for England in 1937 or 1938, wanting to settle in London for good. She made a living there working as a domestic maid. I remember her telling me over and over how impressed she was with Mr. Chamberlain, then British Prime Minister, because she saw him in the cinema news helping a girl in the street collect her poppies which had accidentally fallen from her hands. Poppies were the flowers that reminded the British of the Great War, as the First World War was called before 1939.

Anyhow, when the Second World War broke out in September 1939, Miss Klein made the biggest mistake of her life and returned to Hungary. It was still possible to travel from England to Hungary at the time because Hungary was not yet at war with Great Britain. She came back to Nyiregyháza, to her parents, and made her living by teaching English. Her mother died of cancer just before all the Jews of Nyiregyháza were deported to Auschwitz-Birkenau, as I will relate shortly. Miss Kató Klein was also deported.

After the war, I found out that in Auschwitz she became a *Kapo*, a camp inmate who supervised others for the SS. The story circulated that she was so cruel to the other women inmates over whom she had authority, that with the liberation, the inmates beat her to death as revenge for her behavior.

Kató Klein's teaching-method was to make me learn by heart whole chapters from the various English books she gave me to read, so as to familiarize myself with the way sentences in English literature are formed. I hated this method, although with hindsight I now believe that it wasn't so bad.

In addition to the extra curricular activities just described, I also had to excel in school. Therefore, I usually had all ones. The best grade in those days was one, and the worst was five. You had to get at least three to pass. I am not sure what the consequences were for getting four. My ones didn't include drawing and gymnastics, which for some reason were considered to be "non-Jewish" subjects. I also spent many hours at home reading books, in Hungarian of course. I read all the books of Mikszáth, Jokai, and Karl May, some of them even more than once.

I had many friends and was engaged in various sport activities such as swimming, rowing, ice skating and ping-pong. I loved to go to the cinema once a week, usually on weekends. I went with my friends to see a picture in one of the three movie theaters in Nyiregyháza named Apollo, Urania and another one. I still remember some of my friends' names. The list can be found in the final chapter.

MY MOTHER'S FAMILY

My mother, Ilona, or Iluka as she was called in the family, was born Ilona Bleier on April 7, 1909. Her father was Jenő (Yona) Bleier. He was the head-waiter of the Korona restaurant. The Korona was the biggest and most chic restaurant in town. In addition, it also operated as a card club. The Korona was the place where the "gentry" of the town and its surrounding areas came to dine and play cards. The place still exists and in the nineties an Austrian conglomerate bought it and established a casino and a hotel on the premises, in addition to the restaurant.

So the job of headwaiter was a distinguished occupation and Jenő was treated accordingly. He was born on December 14, 1881 in Szatmar, a small town on the border of Hungary and Transylvania.

Jenő's parents were Zsigmond Bleier (my uncle, Öcsi, Jenő's son, was named after him) and his wife, Regina Mitelman. Jenő had a brother, I think called Elemér, and I believe that the two brothers married two sisters from Banska-Bistrica in the Slovakian region of the then Austro-Hungarian Empire.

Regina Krieser, Jenő's wife and my grandmother, was a beautiful woman. She died of cancer at a very early age in 1929, the year her daughter, my mother, married my father. Regina was around forty years old when she passed away.

Jenő later remarried and his new wife's name was Maria Berger. They lived in Nyiregyháza on Kótai Street. I think this woman was a widow herself because she had a son in his early twenties. I also think that Maria had a sister living there as well with the newly married couple.

While Regina was still alive, the Bleier family lived on Selyem Street at number 7. When he was a boy, the family jokingly labeled my Uncle Öcsi "the phantom of Selyem Street". I believe that this label indicated the fact that Öcsi was a vivacious youngster, full of life and well-liked by everyone.

My grandfather Jenő was a fairly fat man with a bulging stomach who passed away from a heart attack at 2:00 am on November 27, 1934. He was only fifty-three years old at the time of his death.

Jenő had a sister in Nyiregyháza called Katica, or Aunt Katica for me and even for my mother, because Katica was my mother's aunt. Katica was married to Mr. Simkovitz, a silent, lean man. To be silent and to be Katica's husband must have been one and the same thing, if you know what I mean. The story I overheard at home was that Katica's first husband was a prisoner of war in Russia during the First World War and decided to stay in Russia just so that he wouldn't have to be with Katica again. Most probably this was just a vicious rumor, but it indicates how the family viewed Katica.

As I have described above, my mother Ilona (Iluka) was a pretty woman with a perfect figure and also very ambitious for herself as well as for her son. I think that her mother, my grandmother Regina, was a most ambitious parent for her daughter. My mother spoke German, swam, fenced and played the piano. She wanted to become a medical doctor but didn't. I remember even in 1942 or 1943 when she had her appendix removed in Debrecen and I visited her in the hospital, she told me that it is still not too late for her to start studying to become a doctor and that she might go for it in the near future. I remember thinking how odd that such an elderly person would want to start studying anew and enter a career as a doctor. My "elderly" mother was thirty-three or thirty-four years old at the time.

Later, after the war, I found in the Paris home of my Aunt Jolán a picture of me taken as a baby of two or three months, apparently sent by my parents to my father's brother, Miksa, and his wife Jolán. On the back of the picture I read in my mother's handwriting, "This is Karcsika, future MD, pianist, fencer and master of the English language", in essence, everything my mother wanted to be, or maybe what her mother wanted her daughter to become. Thus, ambitions pass from one generation to the next and from there again to the next, and so on.

Is this a good thing? I am not absolutely sure. Maybe, in some sense, it is OK, maybe in some other sense it is not. There is no doubt that my knowledge of the English language, acquired at home while I was still a child, helped me in later life. Maybe it was even critical in my future career in the Israeli Air Force and the Israel Aircraft Industries. Therefore, there are positive aspects to my parents' ambitions. On the other hand, because it was so important in our family for me to excel in school, I might have neglected something more important in my life. I will try to explain. It was very important for me (and my parents!) that I achieve good grades in school, maybe even to be at the top of my class. Therefore, I did my best to live up to their expectations, and, generally speaking, succeeded. But, and this is a very big "but", in the process I think that I also got used to the notion that success in the eyes of the outer world is important, that success in the eyes of the "authorities" is paramount, maybe more important than looking after one's own personal interests, even one's family's. I am "tainted" in this respect. To succeed in my career, not to disappoint my superiors, my bosses, was always very important to me. I was always completely dedicated to my work, loyal to my employers but neglected some of my other duties in life—to my family, and even to myself, such as not giving priority to spending enough time with my daughters and

Asher's mother and her brother, Öcsi

Öcsi and Edit on their wedding day

even devoting time to locate suitable living accommodations in accordance with our standing in society.

My tentative conclusion is this: Let your child develop in the directions of his natural tendencies. Don't try to realize through him or her your own personal ambitions and don't attribute too much importance to achievements which satisfy the existing standards of the various "authorities", whoever they are.

◆

As I have already mentioned, my mother's younger brother was Zsigmond Bleier or most commonly called Öcsi (in Hungarian *Öcsi* means "younger brother"). Öcsi was born in 1911 and was my idol. He was always making jokes, constantly seemed to be in a good mood and, last but certainly not least, on the occasion of my birthdays, but not only then, sent me the most extraordinary presents, like a movie projector, a rifle that shot pellets by compressed air, an electric train, an airplane propeller, which could be wound up by a long and strong rubber band and actually flew, etc. In 1939, Öcsi married Edit Lakos (Löwy) in Budapest and in 1942 my cousin Vera was born.

I looked upon Öcsi and Edit as the ideal couple. I think I wasn't mistaken. They were trying to make the best of their (short) life together. The Nazis murdered Öcsi in January 1945 while he was serving in one of the Hungarian forced labor units for Jews. He was only thirty-four years old at the time of his death.

Öcsi had a movie camera, which in those days was a rarity, and he filmed mostly Edit, but also my parents and me on all occasions when we were together. I am very fortunate that one of these films survived. Gyuri, Vera's husband who is gifted in such tasks and likes to do them, converted this film onto video for me in which I can actually observe my father and mother, Edit smiling and moving and even see myself with Emil Hahn and Robi Vermes fooling around in the huge garden of our home across from the railroad station.

By the way, Edit was called Bebi in her family, maybe because she was younger than her brother Gyuri or maybe because they wanted to pamper her.

MY FATHER'S FAMILY

My father was the youngest child of his parents, Lipót and Rosa Sichermann (her maiden name was Steinberger).

As I have mentioned, my father worked in a company called Futura, which, as I have more recently discovered, was partially owned by the Italian insurance giant, Generali. He was brought to Futura by one of his older brothers, right after he graduated from Kereskedelmi High School. He made a very nice career there. His responsibilities, besides the grain storage facilities, maybe even trading in grain, included overseeing a factory where oil was produced from cornflour and also facilities for storing alcohol.

A curious turn of events advanced my father's career at Futura. The anti-Jewish legislation during the late 1930s and early 1940s forced more and more companies to dismiss their Jewish employees. The same occurred at Futura. Some of my father's Jewish colleagues were let go but not my father. He apparently was so highly regarded that they wouldn't fire him.

On the contrary, when Mr. Jenő Glück, a Jew himself, much older than my father, retired or was forced to retire, my father was promoted to his job. Since this job came with the company's house on Állomás Circle, my father was entitled to have that huge and lovely place. We moved in there in late 1939 or early 1940. I think that it was then that Futura hired Mr. Buji, my father's deputy, who took over from him when my father was fired after the March 19, 1944 German occupation of Hungary.

I am not sure how Mr. Glück regarded the turn of events that led to his retirement and my father's promotion. Did he approve or disapprove of it? There was no social contact between him and his wife and my parents, although I was friendly with the two grandchildren, Istvan and Jancsi Balázs, whose beautiful mother, Erzsébet (the Glücks' daughter), I, one might say, admired.

My father was a kind, good man. He was a little shorter than I am now, but this is as it should be since every generation is a little taller than the preceding one. He had bad teeth, however, which I inherited. I have been visiting dentists all over the world since childhood, making them richer and richer. He also squinted, which I, too, inherited. As a young man, his eyes were operated on, but he still had to wear glasses all his life, which I was spared until the age of nine. He played soccer in his youth and fenced as well. I think he learned to swim only after he married but didn't excel at it. My fingers resemble his and according to Sárkány, my late wife, my stature resembles his.

My father was an optimist, or maybe he just pretended to be one, even when the war started and all the events were favorable to the Germans. Probably he just wanted to give us hope in those difficult years.

Some of my friends consider me a pessimist because of my interpretation of the dramatic events that overpower our lives here in Israel. I don't think I am a pessimist, I believe that my views are realistic. (Doesn't everyone want to believe that he is a realist?) Maybe I am a little bit too much of a realist. Human beings have to dream sometimes and not judge everything purely by logic and reason.

◆

My grandfather on my father's side, Lipót Sichermann, was born in 1860 or 1861 in a little village called Buk Szentmihály, some thirty kilometers from Nyiregyháza. He was a tall, lean orthodox Jew with a short, gray goatee. He became a widow on February 10, 1926 when my grandmother, Roza (Rizel) Steinberger, passed away.

When my parents married, he came to live with them. I suppose that beforehand he lived with my father. While he was alive, our household was kosher. When my parents wanted to taste some non-kosher food, like ham, they would eat it on the little veranda of our house from its package so as not to soil the plates and silver also used by my grandfather. At least twice a day, Grandfather Lipót walked the approximately five-kilometer distance from our house to the orthodox synagogue and back.

I called him *nagyapa*, grandfather. My mother's father was called by the softer sounding *nagyapu*, grandpa. I remember sitting on my *Nagyapa*'s knees, with a mouse with its long thin tail dangling between his fingers, which he smilingly showed me after he had fished it out of a rain-water barrel in our yard. The peculiar thing is that my cousin Laci in Paris had a very similar memory about our *Nagyapa* involving a mouse when he was a little boy in Nyiregyháza. I don't know anything about Lipót's brothers or sisters or whether he had any.

I vaguely remember that we had relatives in Debrecen who spelled their name Zichermann. The old folks there had a small grocery and two sons, a doctor and a lawyer. I don't know how the old Zichermann was related to my grandfather, maybe he was a cousin.

Grandmother Roza's family, the Steinbergers, had a relative, Uncle Vilmos, in Budapest whom I remember visiting with my parents in the early 1940s; they lived somewhere in the vicinity of Vaci Road. After the war, in the summer of 1945, I would be invited there for weekend lunches by Uncle Vilmos's daughter, Manci, who was about thirty years old at the time and an ardent Communist.

The son of this Steinberger family, Gyula, had immigrated in the 1930s to Chile with his wife, and then on to *Eretz Yisrael*[1]. I went to visit them in Tel Aviv some months after my arrival. They lived in a good neighborhood and had a nice, quiet apartment on Gordon Street. They had a daughter with them when I visited. I then lost contact with them, but found out from Laci, my cousin in Paris, that they then lived for a while in Paris where they succeeded in arranging immigration to America and they settled in New York. They owned a small haberdashery in Broadway's black area. I somehow discovered where they lived and one evening in the 1970s, while in New York, I visited them in their Manhattan apartment. They lived in one of those terrible apartment buildings, located in a dangerous, mostly black and Puerto Rican area of the city.

Their morale was low and, sure enough, I later heard that one of the women of the family (I am not sure whether the wife or the daughter) committed suicide by jumping from the window of their apartment. This is the tragic story of a man and his family who couldn't find their proper footing either in Hungary, Chile, Israel or the U.S.

♦

The Sichermann grandparents had, I believe, ten children out of whom five died at birth. Out of the five who survived, there were four boys and one girl. Maybe I am mistaken, and Lipót and Roza only had four surviving children since I don't have a fifth name nor do I know anything about such a person. I only know that the oldest brother, who might have been this fifth son, or maybe Uncle Miksa, introduced my father to Futura when my father graduated from Kereskedelmi at the age of eighteen.

1   The Land of Israel, then under British rule. Also called Mandatory Palestine.

Besides my father, the other children boys were Miksa, whom I have just mentioned, who immigrated to Paris with his family in the late 1920s; Jenő who died after the First World War in Kaló (near Nyiregyháza) where he was hospitalized because of the battle shock he suffered during that war; and Margit, who, because she was the only girl among three or four boys, was pampered by all in the family.

In the 1920s, Margit married Jenő Ungar, a Jewish farmer who lost all his wealth because of his brother's card debts that had to be paid. Jenő had a son from a previous marriage called Joe. After marrying my Aunt Margit, they had a son, Béla, nicknamed Becike, or Ben as he was later called in the USA. Later, when they were already in Wilkes-Barre, Pennsylvania, they had a daughter, Maxine. Jenő passed away some years after Maxim was born.

During my first visit to America in the spring of 1967, I traveled to Wilkes-Barre to meet Aunt Margit, Joe, Ben and Maxim and all of their family. Margit was in her seventies and kept mixing me up with my father. In 1967, I was thirty-seven years old, which was similar to my father's age in 1931 or 1932 when Margit and her family left Hungary for the US. I must have looked like him as she probably remembered him from that time. The "mix-up" was thus somewhat understandable. Anyhow, the impression I got was that Aunt Margit was the brightest person in my American family,

I liked Ben instantly during those few days in the spring of 1967. Ben and Beth, his wife, already had four daughters who were quite young at the time. I found him to be a well-meaning, good-hearted and simple-minded person. He was making a living and providing nicely for his family by selling electrical appliances to people whose credit rating was low and therefore couldn't get regular financing for their purchases. Ben himself provided the necessary funding to his clients.

He had a van with which he delivered purchases directly to his clients, making daily rounds around Wilkes-Barre. Because of his unique type of clientele, Ben ran a more than normal risk of not being paid; he had to compensate for this extra risk by building higher profit margins into his prices. According to Ben, however, he seldom had default problems. He told me that he was selling to people whom he had known for years.

I wasn't surprised to find Ben a little simple-minded because I remembered the story told to me by my parents about him (who was still Becike, at the time) concerning a game he played with me while the Ungars were still in Hungary. Becike must have been a little boy of six or seven and I was just a baby.

It appears that Becike, who was brought up on a little farm near Nyiregyháza, used to play a very unique game with the peasant boys there. The boys put one of their playmates in a bucket and then lowered it into one of the wells in the fields so that the bucket with the child was just about inserted in the water. When the boy in the bucket had enough of the water, he hollered and was then pulled up by his friends.

So one day, as the family legend goes, while visiting our home with his parents, Becike was somehow left alone and unattended, with me, a three or six-month-old baby, in his charge. Becike decided to play with me the same game he used to play with the peasant boys of his age.

In our backyard there was also a well and a bucket attached to a chain to provide water for our household. Becike placed me in the bucket and was about to lower me into the water, most probably drowning me in the process, when our parents, in panic, noticed that neither Becike nor I was around. They found us just in time with me already in the bucket about to be lowered into the well. I never brought up this story with Ben when we met as grown-ups, and I doubt whether he even remembered it.

Anyhow, I liked Ben. He had a soothing influence on me. We took long walks in the forests surrounding Wilkes-Barre, chatting, although because of his peculiar simple-mindedness I sometimes wasn't sure whether he was joking or really meant what he was saying.

Maybe Ben was sharper than I believed him to be. Some years after he passed away, I met Mark, his grandson, when he visited Israel with a Jewish youth group. Mark told me that Ben had made a million dollars on the stock exchange in addition to the four houses he bought for his daughters.

I remember the story told by my parents, that when the Ungars immigrated in 1931 or 1932 to the USA, my parents loaned them 200 or 300 dollars from my mother's dowry. It was agreed that after Jenő Ungar and Aunt Margitwere settled in America they would reimburse the loan and would try to obtain the necessary documents for my parents and myself to join them there. Nothing came of this, most probably because of the difficulties the Ungars, as new immigrants, encountered in America, where the population was struggling to survive during the Depression.

When the Germans occupied Hungary, my parents had me remember all the above information, even the address of the Ungars in Wilkes-Barre. Of course, when we finally met in 1967, neither I nor the Ungar family ever mentioned this loan of 200 or 300 dollars. Maybe I was the only one who remembered it. I suppose the younger generation like Ben or Maxim didn't even know about it. I wasn't about to poison our "newborn" relationship by bringing it up. Also, I knew that Aunt Margit had made inquiries after the war about my parents and me, which was very touching and for which I was indeed thankful.

CHAPTER 2

SEPARATION AND SURVIVAL

THE UNFOLDING DISASTER

As of April 5, 1944, all Jews in Hungary had to have a yellow star sewn to the front of their clothing. Its size, location and stitching were precisely prescribed. I was wearing the yellow star when I took the tram to the Gymnasium for my final examinations of the year. The school year ended early in 1944 because all school buildings were requisitioned as German army barracks. In those exams, I got 1s in all subjects, which I didn't think I deserved because, by my own standards, I hadn't excelled in those exams, definitely not in all the subjects. Maybe the head teacher of my class, Mr. Gacsányi, knew what was awaiting me and this was his way of showing sympathy.

Mr. Gacsányi's son, a very gifted child, was also in my class. Today, in Israel, we would call him a *yoram* (geek). He was a real *yoram*. Later, I found out that he became a nuclear scientist, which didn't surprise me at all. This Gacsányi boy was the only gentile in my class who wasn't openly antisemitic.

I heard that just before the Germans entered Hungary in 1944, Mr. Gacsányi told a group of his history students that Hungary, during its long history, was less threatened by invasion from the East, e.g., Russia, but rather was endangered from the West, by which he must have meant Austria or Germany.

41

I don't know whether he made such a statement before his class, but if so, it testifies to his extraordinary courage.

After the war, the principal of our gymnasium was indicted for being a Nazi sympathizer. I attended the court hearings and I saw Mr. Gacsányi approach the principal during one of the recesses and warmly press his hand. The principal was extreme right in his Hungarian politics and a Nazi sympathizer, but also a very gifted person with great knowledge of Hungarian literature. Seeing this handshake, I thought to myself that Mr. Gacsányi is a courageous man who is neither afraid nor ashamed to demonstrate, for everyone to see, his loyalty to an old colleague, just as in the past he wasn't afraid to express his views about the Germans when such a display of rational thinking was extremely dangerous.

By mid-April, the Hungarian authorities were assembling the Jews from neighboring villages into Nyiregyháza. Some of them were brought to the Orthodox synagogue. We had two synagogues in Nyiregyháza, one Orthodox and the other Status Quo. Later, the German troops blew up the Status Quo synagogue after having used it as a stable for their horses. The Orthodox synagogue survived the war.

One evening at home, I saw my father crying. I had never seen him crying before. He was telling my mother about the scenes he had witnessed in the Orthodox synagogue—about the miserable conditions that the Jews from the villages had to endure. He was crying and saying that not since he had seen his brother hospitalized in Kaló had he seen such misery. Little did he (or we) know what was really awaiting us.

INTO THE GHETTO

The day came at the end of April, when we were to be taken to the ghetto. I am overcome with great anger when I think back on how this ghetto operation was organized. To make it nice and easy for them, the Hungarian authorities demanded a list of all the Jews in Nyiregyháza, including their exact addresses, from the office of the Jewish Community, which became the Jewish Council, with Mr. Fischbein at its head.

This information was duly supplied to them. It was, therefore, no problem for the Hungarian gendarmes to come and collect all the Jews from their homes and take them to the ghetto. Of course, even without the cooperation of the Jewish Council, the Hungarian authorities could have organized by themselves the list of Jews, but it would have been more difficult for them. They might have missed some families; it might have taken more time. It should not be forgotten that the Soviet Army was already approaching the gates of Hungary and any delay in the evil schemes perpetrated against us could have been life-saving.

Waiting for the gendarmes to come, I was playing alone in our dining room. Our house opened onto a beautiful garden of flowers and bushes. There was also a bigger garden of fruit trees and grapes. In addition, my mother had a small chicken enclosure with tens of chickens providing dozens of eggs daily, which she sold for her "pocket money". We called it "egg money" in the family. The house and gardens occupied a terrain of some 20,000 square meters. So now we were to leave these beautiful surroundings where I felt so secure and protected.

The gendarmes arrived a little later than the time specified and then ordered us to leave with them immediately.

Outside, there was a carriage leased to us from my father's workplace. We put our belongings, such as we were allowed to take with us, onto the carriage and because there was enough space left, my mother went to sit there too. The gendarmes, who were busy sealing the house, noticed her sitting on the carriage when they came out of the house. To my astonishment, I heard them shout at my mother, "Who allowed you to sit there? Get off immediately." Nobody had ever shouted at my mother before, not in my presence at least.

This shouting and the message it conveyed, made me understand more than anything else before, the change in our status in this new world, which had suddenly erupted around us. My mother got off and we all started our march of around two or three kilometers to those few streets in midtown where the ghetto had been established.

We were allocated a tiny little space in one of the houses on Körte Street. There were a number of other families also compacted into the same small apartment; even in our room there were additional families. Our precise place in the ghetto was organized in advance by the Jewish Council.

The activities of the various Jewish Councils in German-occupied Europe were, and still are, constantly debated among Jews in the post-

Holocaust years. I suspect that the easy round-up of Nyiregyháza's Jewish population and dragging them into the ghetto was facilitated by lists containing our names and addresses that probably existed in the files of the local Jewish community before March 19, 1944. What if these Jewish leaders had destroyed the files containing information about the Jewish population? It might have made it more difficult and time-consuming to round up the Jews and take them to the ghetto. After all, the Soviet Red Army was already approaching the Carpathian Mountains. Of course, the names and addresses of the whole population of Nyiregyháza were kept and constantly updated by the Hungarian police, so it is not that the Jews could have escaped identification forever, but some time might have been gained.

Another aspect of this impossible situation was brought up during the famous trial of Malkiel Gruenwald versus Yisrael (Rezső) Kasztner in the mid-1950s in Tel Aviv. What if Kasztner, instead of negotiating with Eichmann, had somehow alerted the Jews in the various ghettos about the fate awaiting them in Auschwitz-Birkenau. Would it have made a difference? I am not sure. I doubt it a bit, but maybe it could have made some difference to a handful of Jews with more than average initiative and courage who would have risked trying to escape. But to escape to where? The vast majority of the Hungarian people had no empathy at all towards the fate of the Jewish population, even bitterly hated them. Only a handful of Hungarians in the whole country actively assisted Jews.

Even more than sixty years later, when I know precisely what did happen in reality, it is still a dilemma for me, as to the right course for the self-appointed leaders, like Kasztner, to follow. Should they have tried to alert the Jewish population to the fate awaiting them or was it right to try to save even a handful of Jews by negotiating with the Nazis? So how can we now, in the safety of our homes, after more than half a century, blame people like Kasztner, who then, in 1944, in the midst of those terrible events and constant mortal danger, had to make fateful decisions on behalf of tens and even hundreds of thousands of Jews?

Anyhow, let's return to the facts in the spring of 1944. There was a fence around the ghetto in Nyiregyháza and there were guards posted at the gates not allowing anyone unauthorized to leave or enter.

What was my biggest worry at that time? You won't believe it, but my worry was how I would be able to go to the cinema on the weekend if nobody

SEPARATION AND SURVIVAL   45

was allowed to leave the ghetto. Maybe I was lucky that I didn't understand the reality of our situation. Not realizing what was really going on, helped me, I think, even in Auschwitz, as I will relate later.

In the beginning, we still had food to eat in the ghetto from the stuff we had brought from home, so I wasn't suffering from hunger. I had my friends there (all my real friends were Jewish). Therefore, for me, the situation in the ghetto was bearable even though, at the time, the grown-ups wouldn't have agreed with such an analysis of our situation.

One of my mother's close friends, Ili Horowitz, even got married to her not-so-long-time suitor, whom we nicknamed Keszege, although this was quite close to his real name. This alias indicated in Hungarian that the man was very skinny. The couple had been introduced to each other by my parents who must have enjoyed such matchmaking because I know of at least two other couples they brought together. The reason for this particular, urgent marriage in the ghetto was that most people were thinking that whatever happens in the future, families are going to be allowed to stay together and bachelors might have to struggle alone. It was also considered that a married woman would be more protected from potential atrocities than a spinster.

As it happened, Ili Horowitz returned from Auschwitz after the war but her young husband didn't. She remarried a young tailor and together they immigrated to France where her new husband's brother had a small business. They found peace and happiness there. I visited them in the 1970s together with Jolan and Jenő, who knew them. Ili, her husband and their sons lived and worked in a small town on the outskirts of Paris.

There were rumors, which turned out to be true, that some families committed suicide rather than move into the ghetto. Such was the case with an MD, Dr. Kain, who poisoned himself, his wife and his daughter. I knew the daughter, Ági; she was a year younger than me. Ági was a gifted, pretty, quiet girl who maybe squinted a little. Later, I also found out that the Balázs family did the same. They had a pharmacy in the town so they had access to poison just like Dr. Kain. The Balázs family had two sons. The older son was one year older than me and the younger son, Jancsi, was a year younger. I used to go to their house to play. The mother, Mrs. Balázs (maiden name, Erzsi Glück), was a beautiful woman. She was the daughter of Mór Glück, my father's predecessor in his work at Futura.

I have often wondered to what degree those parents who committed suicide, and convinced their children to do the same, were justified or not, in taking such a fatal decision. For sure, the Kain and Balázs families didn't delude themselves; they didn't want to lie to themselves about the fate they must have known was awaiting all of us.

True, as it turned out, all the Jews of Nyiregyháza ended up in Auschwitz. Most of them were murdered there or perished in other concentration camps. All young or young-looking, and thus unlucky, children were put to death by the Germans upon arrival. I don't know of any child from Nyiregyháza younger than me who survived the deportation. Only some of the boys and girls, born in 1930 or earlier, managed to stay alive in the various concentration camps.

Therefore, those suicide victims who would have gone to their deaths in Birkenau or perished in one of the concentration camps later, were spared that terrible fate, and at least died by the loving hands of their parents, in the "comfort" of their own homes. Who can judge such parents who took it upon themselves to so decide for their children? Not I, for sure! It must have been pure hell to make such a decision!

TRANSFER TO CAMPS

Several days after having settled into the ghetto we were notified that because of the danger of various diseases, which might develop and spread due to the congestion and lack of proper sanitation in the ghetto, which was located in the center of town, we were going to be transferred to camps in the countryside around Nyiregyháza.

On another beautiful spring morning that year, we were led in long columns, Jews of all ages, women and men, children and the elderly, through the main streets of our town to Nyírjes, approximately four to five kilometers away. I clearly recollect the streets of our town and its main square around the Catholic church packed with gentiles, our neighbors and acquaintances, friends of yesterday, who were cheering and laughing and making all the right noises to demonstrate how happy they were that the Jews were thus being humiliated.

Nyírjes consisted of a few small peasant huts. Nearby, the Hungarian gendarmes had erected a camp surrounded by wire fences. Our accommodation consisted of about a two-meter rectangular spot per person on the ground inside a shack originally intended for drying crops. The gendarmes were very cruel. All the time, they searched for hidden money and jewelry, behaving very savagely in the process. Their favorite method to "encourage" the victim to reveal where the real or imagined "treasure" was hidden, was to tie both his hands behind his back and then raise him by attaching a rope to his wrists so that he would hang in the air with his weight pulling down on his arms. This was surely very painful. I never experienced it personally, but we were all forced to watch the suffering of the person being crucified, sometimes for hours.

Every day I volunteered, together with my friends, to go to work. This was the only way to escape the boredom and depressing atmosphere of the camp. In the early morning hours we were marched, surrounded by armed gendarmes, to the town's school building belonging to the Greek Catholic Church where some of the looted belongings of the Jews, mostly from the surrounding villages, were stored. We had to sort out and properly arrange these possessions, which later were either sent to Germany, sold, given to the local population, or stolen.

By marching into the town with my friends every day, working there and then marching back to the camp again, I at least escaped the dreary daily life in the camp. Those others, including my parents, who stayed in the camp during the day, had to endure the boredom of not doing anything and also to suffer the cruelty of the gendarmes.

TRANSPORT TO SOMEWHERE

We realized that our stay in Nyírjes was only temporary. In addition to Nyírjes, there was another similar camp not far away, at a little farm called Harangod.

We believed that we were to be taken to Germany. According to the rumor circulating, most probably promulgated somehow by the Germans, we were to travel to Thuringia, one of the provinces of Germany. We also "knew" that we would work there in agriculture and therefore have plenty of food and that the families, of course, would stay together.

Conditions as they were in Nyírjes seemed to be so terrible that we were actually looking forward to the transports to Germany to begin... and the transports started. The first transport didn't include us. We were scheduled for the second. After the war, I found out that all together there were three transports from Nyírjes and two from Harangod. My greatest worry was that my family and I leave on the same transport as the family of my best friend, Pista Klein.

I tried to remember when Pista Klein became my best friend. We knew that in childhood, maybe later in life as well, best friends rotated from time to time. So, let's say for instance, the day before yesterday Robi Vermes was my best friend and then yesterday Pista Lipkovits or Zoli Schwartz or Gabi Mosckovitch and today again it is Pista Klein. However, being best friends with Pista Klein remained constant and for at least a year or two we were real friends. He joined *Hashomer Hatzair* before me where, among other useful things, he was taught to box.

Pista was smaller than me and I remember my surprise once when I jokingly hit him, he reacted and quite easily succeeded in neutralizing me with measured semi-professional blows of his fists. He was somewhat of a snob, which made his friendship towards me even more valuable. I must have been a snob as well.

We went to Polgari together and were the only Jewish boys there in the fall of 1943, having taken the compulsory tests in Latin and other subjects for acceptance to the Gymnasium for the fourth grade. We studied together with the same teacher. During the summers, we would swim together in the Sóstó where his parents once even rented a small apartment. One summer, we went to swim in the Bujtos because in that year the Sóstó was out of bounds for Jews. I also remember us ice-skating during the winter.

We really had to stick together in the Gymnasium in 1943–1944 because, besides Andris Citrom, we were the only Jewish students in a class of approximately fifty, most of whom were fiercely antisemitic. Andris Citrom's father was an attorney and Andris was considered to be a snob by the other boys. Citrom in Hungarian is lemon and, funnily, Andris had a sour expression. He didn't have many friends, although from time to time I went to play with him in their home on Bocskai Street.

Andris was a "regular" student at the Gymnasium, while Pista and I were "private" students. A regular student had the benefit that he only had to take oral tests limited to current material, while a private student had to take a written test at the end of the year from all the subjects and material covered.

♦

My family was not on the first transport to leave Nyirejes and since Pista Klein and his parents weren't on it either I was satisfied. Then came the day of the second transport. My family and I were included in this transport, but, in the turmoil, I lost track of whether Pista and his family were there as well. After Nyírjes, I never saw him again. He must have been put into the gas chamber, together with his mother, immediately after arriving in Auschwitz.

His father, Adolf Klein, survived Auschwitz. I saw him in Nyiregyháza after the war and also in Israel in later years. When I saw him on the street in 1945 near the municipality building, he didn't address me at all. He was very thin, like all survivors, and he seemed to be depressed, like all the parents who returned only to find that members their families hadn't. In Israel, I talked with Adolf while attending one of the yearly remembrance services for the Jews of Nyiregyháza and its neighboring villages. I reminded him that Pista was my best friend, and he said that he remembered that. I was in my Air Force uniform when we met. It must have hurt Adolf to realize that, but for the Holocaust, Pista would by then have been a grown man with a family, just like me.

I am convinced that every parent who survived the Holocaust but lost a child, suffers constantly, every day of his life, and doesn't need to be reminded of his loss. It was obviously very painful for Adolf and it was painful for me as well.

I remember from time to time dreaming and crying about Pista Klein even as late as 1951 when I was studying in Henlow, England, at the Royal Air Force Academy.

Laci Klein, Pista's older brother, was a gifted violin player. I remember both of us waiting for our separate turns to play during one year's final concert, which Mrs. Führer organized. He was invited to accompany one of the student piano players on the violin. Laci survived the war after serving in one of the Jewish forced labor units of the Hungarian military. I have met him in Israel; we even flew once on the same flight to Europe. Laci didn't seem to want to dwell on the past. As a matter of fact, he hardly wanted to recognize me and speak to me at all.

♦

But let's return to Nyírjes and the spring of 1944.

It was a long walk from Nyírjes to the railroad in Nyiregyháza. In this march we were surrounded by a number of Hungarian gendarmes but only a handful of German SS soldiers. There were some local men and women lined up on both sides of the street as we passed through and this time I don't recall noticing much demonstration of joy. I admit that here and there I even noticed tears being wiped off by some of the peasant women who were looking at us as we slowly moved in the direction of the railroad station.

I saw the Hahn family at the corner of their house on Szarvas Street, gently and sadly waving to us. When I returned from Auschwitz on March 5, 1945, the Hahns took me in and I stayed with them until the summer of 1945 when the head of the family, Dezső Hahn, passed away. I will discuss this later.

We were finally approaching the railroad. To my surprise, we weren't heading in the direction of the regular railroad station opposite our house, but towards a side site one or two kilometers from the station. When we finally got to this site, I was astonished to see no passenger train waiting for us, such as those I used to travel in before, but only a long row of freight cars.

We were herded quickly into the tightly packed cars. Men were there from the Jewish Council and were authorized to distribute water. I remember one of the men, Mr. Gruenfeld, the father of my friend, shouting, "This is Karcsi Sichermann, my son's friend. I have to give him water."

In the car into which my parents and I were pressed, there was Mr. Schwarzkopf, in his fifties, and his wife. Mr. Schwarzkopf was a much respected person in the community. He used to be my Uncle Miksa's friend; Miksa and his family had immigrated to Paris, as I mentioned earlier.

My parents and I had gone from time to time to visit the Schwarzkopf family. I liked to go there despite the order and tidiness one had to strictly observe, with all the chairs, armchairs and sofas covered when we visited. They had the biggest Maerklin set you could imagine. Maerklin was the dream toy of all boys. It consisted of metal strips, hinges, bolts and nuts with which to build machinery of all kinds. Besides the hardware, a Maerklin set consisted of software as well, i.e., blueprints of the machinery one could build. The Schwartzkopf's set even had an electrical motor to drive the crane, tractor or automobile one had constructed. This wonderful Maerklin set used to belong to their son who was already a young man and no longer at home.

The Schwartzkopf's also had a grown-up daughter. During the war, for some reason unknown to me at the time, she returned from France, bringing with her a Siamese cat and also some information about our relatives there from whom we hadn't heard since the outbreak of the war. In France, she lived in the non-occupied zone governed by the Vichy regime of Marshal Pétain. This part of France was later taken over by the Germans and it was then that she returned to Hungary.

Mr. Schwarzkopf suffered from diabetes and therefore had his insulin injections with him in the freight car. He explained to us that he needed these injections to survive. When we got to Auschwitz (instead of Germany), he successfully passed Dr. Mengele's selection but later when we were taken to the showers, his insulin was discovered and he was sent directly to the gas chambers.

Well, we were each crammed in the car with hardly a spot large enough to sit and the train started to move. I remember one conversation among the "passengers" very clearly. The discussion was about the endurance capacity of man as created by God. The optimistic consensus of those participating in this exchange was that "a human being has more strength than a horse when it comes to survival."

There was a very small window, more precisely a crack in the panel of the freight car, and I was located adjacent to it. Therefore, I recall seeing signs indicating that our train was passing through the stations of Kassa (Kosice) in Hungary and later Tarnów in Poland.

Now something was obviously wrong. According to our information and delusion, we were supposed to be traveling west in the direction of Thuringia and here we were traveling to the north and even a little to the east. Why? Why? So we found a "logical" explanation: "The reason for this 'rerouting' is the bombardments, which most probably render some of the rails westward out of order. Therefore, our train has to circumvent the damaged rails." Our capacity for self-deception (*Iden Villen Azoi*) was working overtime.

We had left Nyiregyháza in the afternoon of May 26, and arrived at our destination two days later, at midday Sunday, May 28, 1944. Before arriving at the camp itself, our train stopped for a while at the regular railroad station of a town called Auschwitz, whose name we had never heard before.

"WORK WILL MAKE YOU FREE"

The train started to move again but came to a stop a few minutes later. I looked out from my window crack, twisting my head to better see the surrounding area, and noticed that we were parked outside a wire-fenced area interspersed with watchtowers as far as I could see.

"What is this place? Where are we?" was on everybody's mind. "Why are we stopping all the time? Thuringia is still far away from here. This for sure cannot be our final destination." Then the train moved again, entering a gate and came to a stop. Through my crack, I observed scenery unimaginable to a normal person.

We were in the midst of a camp. As far as I could see there were wire-fenced areas, watchtowers, guards and, most astonishingly, a multitude of people dressed in blue and black striped pajamas. There was noise, loud ear-deafening noise.

We had just arrived in Auschwitz-Birkenau! This was not Thuringia with its clean air and farmland. This was hell. I was thinking that there must have been some mistake. We were not supposed to be here.

The wagon car door was suddenly thrown open from the outside and several striped pajama-wearing men jumped in, shouting, "*Schnell, schnell, raus, raus.*" in German, "Quick, quick, out, out."

One of these men asked my father in Yiddish pointing to me, "Wie alt?" (How old is he?). My father answered, "*Verzehn.*" (He is fourteen.) The man said to my father, "*Sug sechtzen.*" (Say he is sixteen.) I didn't comprehend the reason for this advice; maybe my father did, but it was well given, as we were to understand a little later.

We were told, or to be more precise, ordered in a high volume bellow, "*los, los, schneller, schneller*", "get going, get going, faster, faster", to move promptly and leave all our belongings behind in the car. "Don't worry, your belongings will be brought to you later", we were told. They placed long wooden planks to connect the freight car and the ground and, amidst all the noise and shouting, we descended.

At the other side of the rails there were also several camps where we saw men, women and children together, some of them even wearing normal clothing. I found out after the war that these were Czech Jewish families that the Germans didn't separate at the start but suddenly one morning, later in the summer of 1944, took all of them to the gas chambers. This happened after the majority of the Hungarian transports had arrived in Birkenau.

But human nature, as it is, looks for some hope, any hope to hold onto even in the midst of hell. So we, at the time of our arrival in Birkenau, felt relieved seeing people resembling "normal" families, parents and children together. Come to think of it, the fact that these Czech families were conveniently quartered beside the railroad tracks was no accident. It was deliberate. The SS wanted to delude the arriving, mostly Hungarian, Jews into believing that their families would also be allowed to stay together. It was another trick designed to facilitate the train-disembarking selection procedure of the SS.

Having descended from the car, we were ordered to form two lines, one on the right for the women and another on the left for the men. About to be separated, my mother and father, who must have understood by now the reality of the situation, cried and kissed passionately. They had forgotten that only a few hours earlier in the train they had had some silly argument and were shouting at each other about not being together on arrival in Thuringia.

So I went with my father to the left and my mother went to the right.

Our line moved slowly. There were SS officers standing at the front of the line and we were advancing to face them and be scrutinized. These SS men were playing the role of God or the devil, deciding who would live and who wouldn't. When our turn came, none of them asked my age and sent both of us, my father and me, to the side of the lucky ones, those who were being allowed to stay alive, at least for the present. As we found out the next day, my mother also survived this first "selection" procedure.

I wasn't very frightened at the time. Of course, I didn't comprehend that I might have been sent to my death just as nonchalantly as I was allowed to live. As a matter of fact, I fully understood what had been happening in Birkenau—the gas chambers, crematoria, etc.—only when I returned to Nyiregyháza in March 1945. Of course, I overheard even on our first day in Birkenau the old-timer *Häftlings*, or inmates, telling us that the only way to escape from this place was "through the chimney". They meant that only by dying and becoming smoke after cremation does one leave Birkenau. I listened, heard this information but didn't really understand what I was hearing. I saw the smoke and fire curling up from the tall chimneys of the crematoria and saw the open graves but didn't realize what it all meant. I was really lucky to have been so naive.

After the selection process, we were told to wait at the side together with all the other lucky ones who had passed this most crucial test of their lives. There was a mound about two meters high on our right side where SS soldiers were leisurely sitting, laughing and talking to us. A "friendly" atmosphere reigned, or so it seemed to my naive state of mind. The SS were shouting to us joyfully, "Did you bring good Hungarian salami?" and then, "Throw me your jewelry; you won't be needing it anyhow."

After a while, we were ordered to start moving.

On our way, we passed the camp orchestra, which was playing some classical music. I think the orchestra was composed of women only. I found out after the war that this Birkenau orchestra was located adjacent to the gas chambers. The cynical purpose of the classical music was to create a soothing atmosphere at this site of death. We marched on until we reached a long structure, which we were ordered to enter.

Inside this barrack, instructions were given to remove all our clothing and to take with us only our shoes. We were to be disinfected and given a shower. Our clothes would be returned to us later. I, like all the others, obeyed and, together with my father, we undressed. All this was performed quietly in a not too tense atmosphere.

Suddenly, I heard shouting and not far away from me a person dressed like a *Häftling* was savagely beating one of the men in our group with a thick walking stick. Why? What had happened? Why the beating? Suddenly, there was terror in the air. My mood changed, and I was alarmed. I wasn't used to seeing a grown-up being beaten. It was nothing extraordinary to witness a child getting a blow from another child or from a grown-up but to witness a grown-up being flogged by somebody made my blood run cold.

We were then herded into another room where barbers sitting on little stools removed all bodily hair from everyone with a razor. The newly shaved parts of our bodies were disinfected with a scorching liquid. Then we were ordered into the showers. After the shower, we lined up again and received the now familiar striped pajamas, including a cap.

By now, it was very late and I was exhausted. We were directed into a large barrack, which was really one large hall without any beds or bunks of any kind. There was nothing at all in this barrack; it was completely empty. My father and I fell asleep right away, luckily not even removing our shoes. As you recall we were allowed to retain only our shoes from home. I also still had my glasses. I had been wearing spectacles from the age of nine. I inherited from my father not only his diligence but also his weak eyes and bad teeth. From my mother I inherited shrewdness and ambition.

Next morning, I awoke feeling that somebody was trying to remove my shoes. There he was, this *Häftling*, not one of ours from the day before, who had somehow sneaked into this barrack and was attempting to steal shoes. I imagine that these more senior and vicious *Häftlings* hoped that the newcomers would be too stunned after their immediate encounter with Birkenau to resist, and in consequence, were easy prey. Regular shoes, from normal life, were very valuable in the camps. The unluckiest *Häftlings* were given wooden Dutch shoes, which was really a death sentence because it was impossible to march and work for any length of time in them. The luckier *Häftlings* were issued normal-looking shoes with the sole made of wood instead of leather. Only a few exceptionally favored *Häftlings*, mostly *Kapos*, or others in similar responsible positions, were given regular shoes. Therefore, it was my good fortune that my father chased the thief away, so that I was able to retain (for the time being anyhow) my own shoes from home.

Suddenly, there was a commotion and we noticed that outside our barrack and behind a barbed-wire fence not more than ten meters away there were some female *Häftlings*. These were the women who, just like us, had survived yesterday's selection process. The women were in the yard, outside their barrack. My father and I tried to locate my mother among them.

Then there she was!

She must have noticed us first and was running behind the fence to see us and so that we could also see her. She raised the piece of cloth she had on her cleanly shaven bare head to show us her condition. I don't know why she felt that she had to show us her humiliation, but I imagine she was deeply hurt by the forceful removal of this sign of femininity and she had to share it with my father. I distinctly felt that she was showing this more to my father than to me. As she was running, I think I heard her shout to my father, "Take care of our son." So at least we found out that she had also passed the first selection and that she was alive. However, that was the last time I ever saw my mother. I don't exactly know what happened to her later, but she didn't survive the camp.

I found out after the war that she had sent a postcard to my Aunt Edit in Budapest. The Germans allowed some Hungarian Jewish *Häftlings* to write to their relatives. The purpose of the letters, as far as the Nazis were concerned, was to mislead and placate the Jews still awaiting their fate back in Hungary in order to make them falsely believe that the deportation was not so terrible.

In this postcard, which I now possess, my mother wrote in German, "*Wir sind glücklich angekommen. Ich bin gesund.*" (We have arrived safely. I am in good health.) It was shrewd of my mother to compose in this way the few words she was allowed to write. From this coded message, Edit understood what my mother wanted to convey, namely that we had arrived at the camp all right together, but now my mother was alone, separated from us.

Later that day, we were moved to the "Gypsy sub-camp" in Birkenau. The name originated from the fact that most of its *Häftling* occupants were Gypsies. The men in charge of us in this camp were all Gypsies.

In every barrack there was a *Häftling* in charge called a *Blockältester*, the barrack elder. This Gypsy *Blockältester* taught us newcomers how to stand in rows of five during the parade called *Appel*; how to soldierly-like remove our caps at the command of *Mützen ab* when the SS soldier made his rounds, etc.

I remember the grown-ups talking among themselves about the Polish Jews we had met since our arrival in Birkenau. We had seen them among the *Häftlings* who unloaded us from the train wagons on that day. The man who cautioned my father about my age was most probably a Polish Jew as well.

Why were the grown-ups discussing the Polish Jews? I think it was because of a bad conscience. Now in Birkenau, we understood the suffering that these Jews had been enduring for the past five years while we Hungarian Jews were still enjoying near-normal lives in Hungary. The Hungarian *Häftlings* were saying among themselves, "We didn't help the Polish Jews as much as we should have, while we still could. They most probably will take revenge on us now that they are the old-timers here and hold 'superior positions'."

Despite this apprehension, I have to admit that in the midst of all the suffering I endured in the concentration camp until my liberation in 1945 I never encountered any mistreatment by Polish Jews because of such feared "revenge".

We were all in the same boat. Our fate was now identical.

◆

There wasn't much for us to do because we were only temporarily in the Gypsy camp, awaiting transfer to our final destination. Therefore, there were many *Appels* including all sorts of exhausting exercises such as leapfrog, push-ups and so on.

During one of these *Appels*, I witnessed a scene so heartbreaking that I will never forget it. We were standing in rows of five as always, when suddenly I noticed Jancsi Fried approaching from the direction of the neighboring barrack. He was two years older and I used to visit him at his home in Nyiregyháza with my friend Emil Hahn. Emil was a good friend of Jancsi. To be more precise, Emil took Jancsi under his protection because Jancsi was a little retarded. He had a very, very flat nose originating, according to the story I had heard, from the time Jancsi was a baby and his grandmother accidentally dropped him. From that accident, Jancsi got his flat nose and apparently some brain damage as well. Jancsi was a good-natured, docile boy with occasional outbursts of anger. Emil assisted him in his studies at Polgari.

Jancsi had a sister, two or three years older, named Martha Fried. She was a pretty, gifted girl who played the cello beautifully. Once, before the German occupation of Hungary, my parents and I were strolling near our house adjacent to the railroad station when we met Martha with her boyfriend. This boyfriend was a gifted orator, a university student, and, at the time, an ardent Zionist. Martha was also a Zionist. I overheard my parents remarking when this lovely couple had passed by, "Well, yes, it is understandable if such young people want to immigrate to the Land of Israel and live there." I think what they meant to say was that it was OK for them, a young couple, to go to *Eretz Yisrael* but that my parents were too old for such an adventure.

Martha, whom I liked and admired, didn't return from deportation but I saw her boyfriend in Nyiregyháza in 1945. Later, I heard rumors that he abandoned the Zionist idea and became a member of the Hungarian Communist Party.

Jancsi's father was a graduate engineer—a very rare profession for a Jew in Hungary in those days. He was the Director of NYVKV, an acronym for the Nyiregyháza's narrow-rail tram service. This was a very distinguished job in our town and Mr. Fried was a highly respected person.

So now, while we were standing at attention during *Appel* in the Gypsy camp in Birkenau, Jancsi Fried approached searching for his father. One has to understand that in Birkenau for any *Häftling* to move from one place to another without a specific command was among the many kinds of disobedience that were punished most severely. Jancsi, of course, because of his mental limitations, couldn't have comprehended the situation. He only wanted to be with his father.

I looked at Jancsi who was just a few meters away. The association I had was of a little innocent animal in distress, looking for the protection of its master. Mr. Fried had no choice but to explain to Jancsi that he had to leave and go back to his barrack. I saw the hurt on Jancsi's face. He couldn't have understood that his father was in no position to help him. I hoped that he didn't feel betrayed by his father. I think I observed acute anguish in Mr. Fried's face, who otherwise was a very composed and confident person.

This scene touched my heart and I will remember it all my life.

◆

We hadn't been given any food for at least forty-eight hours. I was getting very hungry. Miraculously, there were some Jews from Máramarossziget (Sighet; Sighetu Marmaţiei) who, with their healthy sense of survival, hadn't surrendered the bread they had brought with them from the train despite the strict orders to leave everything behind. My father, who noticed them eating their bread secretly, approached and, in Yiddish, begged them to give me, his son, some bread. They didn't even reply to his request. It was as if they hadn't even heard him. It was, of course, very naive of my father to hope that under such conditions someone would share his meager food with a stranger.

Some more time passed before we were given the stuff that passed for food in Birkenau. The truth is that I, who was a growing youngster and at home had consumed huge amounts of food, started to suffer from hunger right then in May 1944; this hunger lasted, with only a few interruptions, until May 1948 when we arrived at Kibbutz Yakum in Israel. There were, of course, days and even months during those four years of hunger when I had enough food but, by and large, I was always hungry. After May 1948, I always had enough to eat, mostly even too much, and the variations were only in the quality of the food.

One night in Birkenau there was a commotion in the block. Personal identification numbers were to be allocated to each of us and this number was to be tattooed on the left arm. You won't believe it, but this news was received with joy.

Why? Because by *Häftling* logic if they took the trouble of providing you with an ID number and even affixed it permanently on your arm, it indicated that they didn't intend to murder you right away. If they wanted to get rid of you soon then why take the trouble of allocating ID numbers and making tattoos? There was a certain logic in this, so everybody was happy.

Not considered real human beings, we were to be recognized only by a number. Each of us was given a number and we lined up for the tattooing. My father, who always stood in front of me in line, was given the number, A-11605, I became A-11606. I still have the number tattooed in blue on my left arm.

A few days later, we were lined up as usual for the morning *Appel* and were marched off. On our way through Birkenau, I saw women *Häftlings* digging trenches. This was also a new sight for me. It was quite unusual to see women doing such hard work in my previous "civilian" life.

Far away, I caught sight of the embankment where we had arrived only a few days before. I saw new arrivals lining up for the selection process. They were still dressed in their normal clothing. It was an unbelievable sight for me. Although only a few days had passed since we had arrived in Birkenau, the impact of this sight was so harsh on me that it seemed as if I had been in Birkenau for months. Observing that there were still people in this world who wore normal clothing, besides SS uniforms and *Häftling* pajamas, was startling. Just as K-Zetnik testified during the Eichmann trial, Auschwitz was not located on this earth—it was another planet.

We marched out of the Birkenau camp and after about half an hour arrived at the gate of another camp. Murmurs went through the rows of *Häftlings*. There it was, the infamous, nowadays universally recognized, sign engraved in an arch on the iron gate, "*ARBEIT MACHT FREI*", which translates as "Work Makes You Free". After the concentration camp, the central desire of my life became to live as a free man in a democratic society. No wonder that even this fraudulent message of possible freedom galvanized us all.

Suddenly our spirits rose. This was an optimistic omen. But do they, the SS really mean it? Of course not! It is a hoax! We knew it was a hoax, but the sons and daughters of Adam and Eve are created so that they will always search for something good to believe in. A drowning man will clutch at a straw to try to save himself.

We went on marching into the camp.

We were in Auschwitz 1. This was the original Auschwitz concentration camp. Birkenau or Auschwitz-Birkenau was erected later and was much larger. It seemed to be a very clean, Prussian-clean, camp.

We were led to a barrack much different from the barracks in Birkenau. This was a two-story building and we were to be accommodated above. The optimism of the *ARBEIT MACHT FREI* sign at the entrance didn't reflect at all the atmosphere reigning inside. You could smell the cruelty in the air.

Then, surprise, surprise. Somebody circulated the rumor that there was a cinema in the camp, which we might be allowed to attend. You won't believe it, but I was such a naive child even then that I was hoping that we would be allowed to go to this cinema. As a matter of fact, I do believe that there was a cinema in Auschwitz but for the SS and maybe the *Blockältesters* and the *Kapos*.

What was awaiting us was not cinema but the merciless reality of our situation.

One day, while still in my barrack, I noticed a young, handsome *Häftling* surrounded by wailing men. It was obvious that the young man was trying to console and encourage them. Suddenly, I realized that the young man was none other than Dr. Aladár Wax, my teacher from home. I didn't recognize him at first because his beard was shaven off and he thus appeared to be much younger than I remembered him. His behavior made a great and positive impression on me.

In the concentration camp, it was mostly every man for himself. To see someone who cared for others and trying to console his fellowmen was exceptional. It might seem a small unimportant event for us now, living a normal life, but there in Auschwitz, in the apparent hopelessness of our situation, to care for others was a real noble act.

Some days after our arrival we were all given an injection in the chest. On the one hand, it was again a good sign that the SS wanted us to live, because otherwise why waste an injection, which costs money. There are simpler and cheaper methods to kill. On the other hand, one never heard of an injection administered in the chest. Injections are given in the arm. But this time the optimists won again. We didn't die from the injection.

ALONE

One of the routines, from time to time, was to line up for various SS officers to select men for transfer to the different work camps. The SS left the able-bodied alive, of course, because they needed our labor.

One such visit turned out to be devastating for my father and myself. An SS officer came to select men for his particular labor camp. We lined up and I maneuvered as usual to position myself just behind my father. The SS officer passed each and every person in the barrack and decided whom to take with him. A *Häftling* clerk followed the SS officer and recorded the number on the arm of the selected person.

They got to my father. The SS made a sign for the clerk to note my father's number. Then the SS officer passed me without asking the clerk to write down my number. The meaning of this was that my father would be taken to a particular camp without me, and I would be separated from him, remaining all alone for whatever fate awaited me.

I have been pondering this event for years. Did my father do the right thing by not saying anything about me to the SS officer who selected him but not me? Was he supposed to ask that his son go with him as well? It was logical to assume that my father was selected to be taken to a work camp and not to the gas chambers.

Was the reason he didn't say anything because he was too frightened to speak up? Or maybe he didn't speak up on my behalf because he was standing in front of me and the SS officer came to him first and only then to me, so my father couldn't have guessed that he was not going to select me as well? Or maybe my father was so shocked that he was unable to think clearly at that critical moment.

And what about me? Why didn't I speak up? When the SS officer passed my father and his number was taken down by the clerk I should have realized that my father might be taken to some destination without me. Why didn't I speak up? Why didn't I say to the SS officer looking at me that he had just chosen my father, that I am his son and would like to go with him? To be honest, I don't think that I even contemplated the idea of addressing an SS officer.

The atmosphere was one of sheer terror. Nobody dared to utter a sound. You could hear a fly buzzing in the air. We were all terrorized knowing that life and death were just the blink of an eye away. This SS officer who chose the men for his particular assignment had the power to order the immediate execution of anyone without a second thought and his order would have been carried out right away. Therefore, it is no wonder that my father didn't speak up nor should anyone be surprised that I didn't say anything either.

During the long years that have passed, especially after I became a parent and later a grandparent, I have often thought about the suffering then and my father's state of mind in the hours, days, weeks and maybe months after our separation in Auschwitz. Maybe he felt that he had abandoned me to my fate, had left me all alone in the hell of the concentration camp. His conscience most probably bothered him for all the limited number of months he was still allowed to live. In addition, I have wondered, how a man, the head of his family, being aware consciously and instinctively of the traditional "male responsibility" for the well-being of his tribe or family, could endure such a situation in which he was prevented by forces much beyond his control to fulfill his responsibilities.

How both my parents must have suffered not knowing anything about the fate of their only child and most probably fearing the worst. How I wish I could have told my father not to blame himself and not to worry for what "fate" had in store for me. After all, it all turned out well for me. I survived the concentration camp on my own, grew up, raised a family and was even fortunate to actively participate in the rebirth of Jewish independence in the State of Israel.

I sometimes wish that I could convince myself to believe in the existence of life after death, somewhere, so I could see him and my mother again and comfort them by demonstrating that despite all the odds, I at least survived.

Anyhow, the fact that I thus came to remain all alone in the concentration camp contributed, in my mind, a certain rationale to my survival. Why? Because I think that in the face of the endless suffering in the concentration camp, any father, in addition to his own distress, was incapable of helping his son and must have felt humiliated because of his powerlessness causing him immeasurable pain. It would have been the case vice versa as well.

I particularly recall a youth from Nyiregyháza, a couple of years older than me, who was there with his father, and whom I later befriended in the concentration camp of Jaworznow, a sub-camp of Auschwitz. Both of them visibly grieved so much in observing each other's sufferings, without being able to help one another, that it nearly drove both of them crazy, and on top of that it created animosity between them as well. To be honest, I have to admit that contrary to this theory, I heard about sisters or relatives who bound together in the hell of the camps, helping each other and thus surviving.

After the selection process, when my father was led away to another barrack, I was so absorbed in my own distress of having been separated from him that I didn't think of the pain he must be suffering. But at the time, when I was left alone in Auschwitz, I was only concerned about my own survival. I felt a near physical pain, as if someone had twisted a knife in my stomach. I constantly suffered from this semi-physical pain for months on end. I don't know when it left me for good, but most probably only after years had passed.

The day after my father was led away, I heard someone calling my name from downstairs in front of our barrack. It was Zoli Schwartz, my friend from Nyiregyháza. How did he dare to stand there outside in the street between the barracks?

In Auschwitz, it was absolutely forbidden to move around on the grounds. Everyone was confined to the barrack where he was quartered. Zoli wasn't one of our group and this was the first time I had seen him since we arrived in Birkenau and then in Auschwitz. It was very clear that he was breaking the regulations and thus endangering himself. Although, such behavior was, one might say, typical of Zoli.

Zoli had been my friend and classmate in elementary school and in Polgari High School. In Polgari, there were two classes for each age group. A student was placed in one of the classes based on the first letter of his last name: from "a" to "l", the student was in class A and from "m" to "z" in class B. That's why Zoli and I were in the same class not only in elementary school but also during the three years that I was at Polgari.

From time to time, I used to visit him in his home. They lived in a little barrack-like house located in a courtyard adjacent to the Roman Catholic church in the center of the town. The Schwartz family was quite poor. The father, Hugo Schwartz, was a thin, even meager, silent person who had a little kiosk where he sold sweets, etc. to the children swimming in the summer and ice-skating in the winter. Zoli's mother, on the other hand, was a well-built, maybe even fat, ambitious and malicious woman. She wouldn't accept what she perceived to be their lower social position because of the father's occupation and economic status. Zoli had a kid sister, Mandi. I was under the impression that his mother, for some reason, wanted me to date her. However, at the time, I already had a girlfriend, Evi Teitelbaum, so nothing came of her matchmaking. Although, even without Evi, I think I wouldn't have considered it seriously. Mandi wore glasses, as did Zoli and I.

Evi didn't wear glasses. She was a silent, well-brought-up girl, one year younger than me. Evi and I went to a dancing class together where we became a "couple", although I forget how this relationship came about. As a matter of fact, there wasn't much to it anyhow. I still remember her face, she was a pretty girl, but I don't recall us talking too much. I do recall that I would step on her toes quite often during the dance lesson. I also remember her pointed, polished, shiny black dancing shoes. Evi's parents were Orthodox Jews, though not fanatically religious.

After my Bar Mitzvah, I had a brief "religious" spell. I laid *tefilin* (phylacteries) in the morning and attended the synagogue for prayers on Friday evening. After synagogue, I would be invited to the Teitelbaum home for the festive dinner. Never in my life have I refused an invitation for a good meal, so every Friday evening I ate with the Teitelbaums. Evi had an older sister, Lila. She was a redhead and had the temperament of one. I liked Lila very much as well.

She was sixteen at the time but behaved like someone much younger; that's why I think she treated me as her equal. It was obvious to me that Evi was her father's favorite. On the whole, the Teitelbaums were a very friendly, honest and kind family. Tragically, neither the parents nor the daughters returned from deportation.

♦

Let's go back to Zoli Schwartz. He had deep blue eyes, which also added to his air of restlessness. He was a quick thinker and even quicker in his gestures and movements; nowadays, one might call him slightly "hyperactive". I remember him as a restless boy, always in motion.

Zoli introduced me to the secrets of masturbation. I remember that at first, I didn't comprehend what he was talking about and only after graphically describing what, how and where did I fully understand what he was talking about.

Zoli was the type of person who didn't know the meaning of fear. This trait of his might explain the fact that he was now standing in front of my barrack in Auschwitz and calling my name. Zoli quickly told me that he and my father were in the same barrack expecting to be transferred at any time to their work camp.

While he was standing outside, he also quickly reported to me about his experiences with the *Poliak* as the Polish non-Jews (or sometimes, even the Polish Jews) were nicknamed. Zoli was the first person to refer to these "superior" *Häftlings*, who held the more responsible positions of *Kapo* and *Blockältester* in Auschwitz, as mere *Poliak*.

Typically, Zoli already knew the ropes and was in on the general picture. He was really fast. Unfortunately, he didn't survive the camps and after this brief encounter in Auschwitz, I never saw him again. After the war, I have often thought back to that meeting in Auschwitz and to the fact that Zoli's hasty nature and fearlessness couldn't have contributed to his chances of surviving.

A little while after Zoli left, I was called again. This time it was my father. I saw him standing before my barrack. He brought me two slices of bread, spread with jelly. He couldn't enter our barrack so someone, I don't recall who, delivered the bread to me. The jelly was already blotted in the bread, indicating that my father had saved it for me for quite some time. This gesture of sharing with me his meager portion of food and also risking punishment by coming to my barrack touched my heart. Maybe I had this feeling of appreciation only later on; at the time, I consumed the bread right away and continued to feel sorry for myself and be absorbed in the grief of my own loneliness.

My father was a softhearted, optimistic, gentle person, a good and clever man. Being softhearted and gentle wasn't among the necessary traits of character for survival in the hell of the Nazi concentration camps. Tragically, he didn't survive, nor did my mother.

Later in the camps, or wherever I found myself, or when a new transport arrived at my camp, I would always look for him, inquire about him, but with no results whatsoever. After those few seconds in front of my barrack in Auschwitz, I never saw him again nor did I find out any reliable information about his fate. I can still see him standing there before my barrack, calling my name with the jelly bread in his hand.

TRANSFER TO SLAVE LABOR

Some days later, all of us still in my section of the barrack were moved to a dark hall with no light whatsoever, to wait for transportation to some labor camp. It was late afternoon when the trucks arrived and we were tightly packed in. The trucks started to move and we were on our way, as we later found out, to Jaworznow. I remember constantly losing my balance when the truck turned, slowed or accelerated. It was completely dark when we arrived after a short journey at this new concentration camp located in the Upper Silesian village of Jaworznow.

Our truckload of *Häftlings* was to be quartered in block no. 6. Waiting there to receive us was the *Blockältester*, himself a *Häftling*, although a privileged one, called Vogel, or *Herr Blockältester* Vogel. He was a Polish Jew who had immigrated to France, where the Germans arrested him with so many other Jews, and eventually shipped him to Auschwitz. In France, Jews from Eastern Europe such as Poland were given "first priority" in deportation to Auschwitz and other concentration camps in the East.

After liberation, Vogel was taken into custody by the Soviets and deported to Siberia. He was eventually released in the 1950s and then suddenly turned up in Israel where, as a suspect war criminal, he was again arrested. I found out about Vogel's arrest from the newspapers and participated in his trial. I informed the court that I was in Vogel's block during the war and so I was summoned as a witness for the prosecution. I later regretted testifying against him when I found out that Vogel was arrested following blackmail by a former *Häftling* who threatened that unless he paid a bribe he would be reported to the authorities. Anyhow, my testimony was very mild. I was asked whether I had seen Vogel kill anyone and I hadn't. I did see him beating people mostly for a breach of discipline, measured by concentration camp rules. I don't recall that he ever hit me.

Vogel got away with a light sentence. The court took into consideration the fact that he had already been incarcerated after the war in Siberia for the same crimes. At the time of his trial in 1954, Vogel was an old and broken man, not at all the person full of vigor that I remembered.

At the time of the trial, I was an officer in the Israeli Air Force and came to court in uniform. I heard Vogel say that he didn't remember the "captain", that he didn't remember me at all. This was not surprising, first because in Jaworznow I was still just a child and also because I had understood that in the concentration camp one had a much better chance to survive by remaining inconspicuous. Like they used to say in the Soviet Union before its demise, "the nail which sticks out gets hit on the head by the hammer."

At the beginning of my internment in Jaworznow, I was often noticed by various officers because of my glasses. To be pointed out in the concentration camp for anything, was always bad. It was easy to select one for the worst kind of tasks by shouting "*Du mit die Brille, komme hier*", "You with the glasses, come here." As time passed my glasses got broken, so although I didn't see very well, my easily identified appearance disappeared.

In Jaworznow, Vogel had a *Pipel*, a young good-looking boy who came from somewhere in Carpatho-Russia, the area of Hungary bordering on the Soviet Union in 1944 (pre-war Czechoslovakia; today in Ukraine). I didn't fully understand in Jaworznow that besides being a personal servant, a *Pipel* was also a sexual object for his master who was usually a privileged *Häftling*. Officially, this particular *Pipel* was helping Vogel in his duties as *Blockältester* and thus didn't have to do slave labor outside the camp like everyone else. However, he gained his privileges mainly because of his other duties, as I have just explained.

I think that I saw this boy, a grown-up after the war, among a group of UJA visitors at Israel Aircraft Industries, although I am not absolutely sure that it was really him.

I knew two other boys in Jaworznow who were *Pipels*. One of them, I forget his name, spoke Hungarian and we were somewhat friendly. He came from a village near Nyiregyháza. He was a pretty boy with rosy cheeks. He tried to convince me to "pretty myself" so as to also be eligible for "Pipelhood". I admit that at the time I didn't understand what he meant. During the calamity of the death march of January 1945, about which I will report later, I saw him among a group of his Greek friends but then he disappeared and I haven't seen him since. I met his father in February 1945 in Kraków, after the liberation. He was inquiring about his son. I told him that I had seen him alive during the death march. I tried to optimize this fact as best as I could, so that the father wouldn't lose hope. However, he already knew that his son was seen alive during the death march, which couldn't, of course, ensure that he had survived the march and its aftermath.

♦

After arriving in Block 6 in Jaworznow, we were registered by the clerks (most clerks in Jaworznow were Czech), their desks having been set up at the block entrance. After registration, we had to wait for Vogel to allocate us a place in the bunks and give each person a blanket.

It was a lengthy procedure. Everyone had to wait his turn for his number to be called. By then, it was already late at night and I was tired. I sat down on one of the lower bunks and fell asleep. Since I was alone, nobody took the pain to wake me when my number was called. I awoke only when Vogel was especially looking for me because my number was the only one not accounted for. I was so terrified of the punishment that I would most probably get that I pissed in my pants. For some reason, Vogel overlooked my "crime" and I wasn't even slugged.

♦

Inside the camp, the big chief among the *Häftlings* was the *Lagerältester*, the Camp Elder and the inmate in charge of the camp. He was a German criminal, a non-Jew. Under him was the *Blockältester*—one *Blockältester* for each barrack. Among the *Blockältesters* there were Poles as well as Jews. In each barrack there were one or two *Stubediensts* in charge of maintaining the barrack.

In addition, there were the *Schreibers*, the clerks who kept all the records of the *Häftlings* and who were somehow influential in arranging privileged workplaces outside the camp, as we shall see later. Most of the *Schreibers* were non-Jewish Czechs.

In the *Krankenbau*, or clinic, you had the chief doctor, who was a non-Jewish German Communist, who at a very critical moment saved my life, as I will relate later. There were also other doctors, most of them Jewish, and their health assistants.

This list, together with the cooks in the kitchen, delineates those privileged *Häftlings* who didn't have to march off to work each day outside the camp.

At the worksite outside the camp, the big chief among the *Häftlings* was the *Oberkapo*. He was a young non-Jewish Polish prisoner—a very cocky type of person. Under him were various *Kapos*, most of them non-Jewish Poles and only a few of them Jewish.

Under the *Kapo*, came the *Unterkapo* and under him, the *Forarbeiter*, a foreman. All these were followed by the ordinary *Häftlings* like me, the slave laborers.

The *Lagerältester*, the *Blockältester*, the *Oberkapo*, and the *Kapo* were recognized by an appropriate band on the upper arm. These were the "officers". The *Unterkapo* and *Forarbeiter* wore their band on the wrist. These were the "non-commissioned officers". Real German organization. Prussia at its worst.

All *Häftlings*, including the most privileged ones, had a number, which was their identity indicator. This number, not one's proper name, was the official ID in the concentration camp. Most *Häftlings*, like me, had this number tattooed on the left forearm. The number was also sewn on one's jacket. In addition, each *Häftling* had an emblem also sewn on the jacket characterizing the reason for his internment: red triangle indicated "political prisoner"; black triangle indicated "saboteur"; green triangle indicated "criminal"; and pink triangle indicated "homosexual".

Jews also had a yellow, upside-down triangle superimposed on the basic triangle, so it formed a *Magen David*, a Star of David.

The responsibility of all the privileged inmates was to make sure that the average *Häftling* worked hard. To achieve this aim, they were encouraged by their superiors to physically intimidate and immediately punish anyone whose work performance didn't seem to be up to expectations. Most of the "officers" fulfilled this task vigorously. Sometimes you found someone even among the *Kapos* who tried to behave like a human being, despite the risk thereby to his privileged status and more. Such a *Kapo* was a French Jew of Hungarian origin by the name of Steg. Actually, he was a cousin of Mr. Steg of Nyiregyháza, an Orthodox Jew who owned a little kosher meat store and whose son was a classmate of mine in elementary school. Neither this Mr. Steg nor his son, however, was in Jaworznow with us. The *Kapo* Steg survived. I remember seeing him after the liberation.

A non-Jewish *Kapo* seemed to have a higher status than a Jewish one. Just before Christmas 1944, the *Oberkapo* and one other Polish *Kapo* disappeared from the camp for a while and then returned. It was rumored that they had been granted some sort of leave, which was an incredible privilege, of course. It could have been true, though, because I noticed that they were on very friendly terms with the SS. In addition, I don't recall seeing any of the non-Jewish *Kapos* participate in the death march in January 1945. The SS most probably released them beforehand or at least let them escape.

◆

The morning after our arrival in Jawarznow, we were marched off to our first day of work. The *Häftlings* of Jaworznow concentration camp were divided into three different groups and marched off to three different locations: the coal mines; the *Gleisbau* to lay train rails; and the power station to erect electric installations. Those *Häftlings* working in the coal mines were quartered in separate barracks and received somewhat better food than the others.

The *Gleisbau* was terrible. It was very hard work, and the SS were nearby, contrary to the camp itself and the power station where they were usually outside the fences and in their watchtowers.

During the long hours of work, the SS were bored and were often looking for some amusement. Such amusement took various forms of cruelty to some unfortunate *Häftling* chosen at random. Once an SS guard decided that one of the *Häftlings* wasn't clean enough. He sadistically knocked him down and started to jump up and down on his stomach. The German shouted repeatedly, "You are not a human being, you are a swine." I remember the face of that not-so-young SS guard. He was wearing glasses and could have passed for a clerk or schoolteacher if one was to meet him wearing civilian clothes in the street. There was genuine loathing in his eyes. It seemed that he had really convinced himself that this unfortunate *Häftling* was not a human being.

Some years ago in Israel, I read the diary of Goebbels, Hitler's Minister of Propaganda. He wrote that the SS in the *Einsatzgruppen* who were carrying out the extermination of the Jews in White Russia and the Ukraine were idealists because they were doing an unpleasant, but highly necessary task, and should be honored for their devotion.

Another terrible cruelty that I witnessed ended with the murder of a *Häftling*. It took place during the summer of 1944 following the arrival of a transport of Jews from the Lodz Ghetto. There was this short, very thin Jew working beside me shoveling coarse sand just like me. He was murmuring something to himself. I remember thinking that he most probably wasn't mentally balanced, understandably so given the conditions these people had had to endure for years in the ghetto and now here. All the recent arrivals from Lodz Ghetto were in very bad shape even relative to us inmates from Jaworznow concentration camp.

One of the young SS guards spotted this Jew murmuring to himself and ordered him to approach immediately. Then the SS man made him stand at attention in front of a tree some twenty to thirty meters away. He then proceeded to target shoot, together with another guard, aiming at this miserable Jew. It didn't take long before he was hit by many bullets and died. After work, we had to carry his cadaver back to the camp because, dead or alive, the number of *Häftlings* returning to the camp in the evening had to match the number marched off in the morning.

Like everyone else, I tried to evade being assigned in the morning to the *Gleisbau* detail but didn't always succeed. The only "non-unpleasant" memory I have from the *Gleisbau* has to do with a pear core. Sometimes during the summer when the SS guards were eating apples or pears, they threw away the core with some of the fruit left on it; once or twice I was able to scramble in time to get a core for myself.

Most of the time, however, I was lucky enough not to be marched off in the morning to the *Gleisbau* and was led to work at the construction site for the power station. I was engaged there during the spring and summer and early fall of 1944, in various manual chores related to the erection of the power station. I dug trenches, unloaded and loaded fifty-kilogram cement sacks, carried cement sacks on my back, mixed and poured concrete, etc. It was hard work with the various *Kapos* and their underlings always at our back hitting and shouting "*schneller, schneller*", "faster, faster".

As I have already mentioned, I learned to speak German starting at the age of five. Therefore, I thought I knew the language. However, in the concentration camp a completely different German was spoken. I mean expressions and words I had never encountered before. For instance, one of the words one heard constantly was *Schweinhund*, which means "swine-dog". What sort of German word was that? I am sure Goethe didn't realize it existed. Another expression was *Saujude* meaning "Jewish pigs". And so on, and so on—a new German Nazi language created by the intellectuals of the Third Reich.

♦

Let's now consider the daily schedule in the Jaworznow concentration camp.

We were woken early in the morning. In the fall and winter, it was still very dark when we had to get up. After organizing the bunk and cleaning the barrack, breakfast was brought in. We had to line up for the food and then sit at one of the tables located in the middle of the barrack. Each table had a *Häftling* responsible for order called a *Tischenältester* or table elder.

The breakfast consisted of either a half or a third of bread and some margarine. In addition, we got a small portion of marmalade or, on some lucky days, a piece of *Wurscht* (sausage). The Germans managed somehow to produce a sausage without much meat as its ingredient. We also got something called tea or coffee, a liquid which didn't resemble any tea or coffee that I knew from home. The more determined among us saved some of the bread to eat later at work.

After breakfast, we had to stand in rows of five at *Appel*. At first the *Blockältester* ensured that everyone was present and that the number of *Häftlings schtimt* (matched up), and then the SS guard who made his rounds of the various barracks arrived. The *Appel* was called by the *Blockältester* for everyone to stand at attention, followed by the *Mützen ab* (caps off) order. The *Blockältester* reported the number of *Häftlings* present to the SS guard in strict military fashion with his cap also removed. The SS guard then went through the rows and ensured that the number reported matched the number of *Häftlings* present.

Appel was always a procedure full of tension and danger, like so many other aspects of life in the concentration camp. The *Blockältester* was nervous, one could sense it. He had to ensure that the *Appel* was swiftly and correctly organized. There wasn't time to waste; we had to be off to work on time and the numbers had to match up. Anyone taking his time and not lining up immediately endangered the *Blockältester* himself by not being ready for the SS inspection, and was severely and immediately beaten by the *Blockältester* in consequence.

After *Appel*, we were split into two units, one for work at the *Gleisbau* and the other for the power station site. Each unit was organized into groups of a hundred men in twenty rows of five men each. In a group which contained less than a hundred *Häftlings* the row before the last was the one with less than five men. We were marched out of the concentration camp where usually the same SS guard counted off the number of *Häftlings* leaving for each destination. These numbers were then re-checked to make sure they would match up when we returned from work in the evening.

At the worksite we immediately began our tasks. During the summer, we worked twelve hours with a short break for lunch. Lunch was brought to us in large containers. Those lucky ones who were ordered to carry the containers from the truck were also those who cleaned them after their contents were distributed to the *Häftlings*. They were lucky because the little soup left in the containers was theirs to swallow before they washed them. The soup was mainly water, it contained very few vegetables, but what there were would accumulate at the bottom of the container; therefore, it was important to ensure that when you got your portion, the person distributing the soup with his large ladle stirred it thoroughly, so that some of the stuff in the water got onto your plate. Every *Häftling* had a plate and a spoon, which he guarded with his life because if he lost his plate he had no way of getting soup. We sharpened the spoon handle and thus used it as a knife as well. Another way to ensure that you got "thick" soup was to maneuver so that you got to the container when its thicker bottom part was distributed. But then, of course, you had to stand longer in line and had no time left for a little rest before going back to work.

During the fall or winter when daylight got shorter, we worked ten hours without stopping and got no food at the work site. The soup was then provided in the barrack after returning from work in the evening.

At the end of the day, the command "*Feierabend*" was heard. This was always a happy moment. Work for that day was over, and we lined up to proceed back to the camp. We were again quickly organized into groups of a hundred and marched back to the *Lager*, as the camp was called in German. We returned exhausted and hungry. Some of the *Häftlings* had no strength left at all and had to be dragged by others. At the gate, we were again counted by the SS guard and after entering we were dismissed to return to our barracks.

There were seven workdays each week with the exception of every second Sunday, which was supposed to be a non-work day. On that day, we didn't leave the camp but, as a rule, weren't allowed to stay inside the barracks either. Those Sunday "rests" were by and large as bad, or sometimes even worse than the regular working days. Why? Because while hoping for a little rest, we were occasionally rounded up for even longer and harder work in the camp itself.

◆

Anyhow, on regular workdays during the fall and winter, we were given our daily portion of soup or the tea-coffee liquid when dismissed. Once in a while, maybe every four weeks, we had to line up to be taken to the showers to wash. On those occasions, a small piece of soap was issued and our clothes were also exchanged for freshly disinfected garments.

Our clothing consisted of a piece of linen which passed as a shirt, pajama type trousers and jacket made of very thin cloth; in the winter, a thin overcoat with blue stripes just like the trousers and jackets. The very lucky and privileged *Häftlings* had real shoes. Others got shoes with wooden soles and the most unfortunate ones were issued Dutch style clogs made completely of wood. It was impossible to march, run or work in such clogs. Therefore, when a *Häftling* was issued one of those, he was actually handed his death sentence.

After someone stole the shoes I still had from home, I was given a pair of the wooden-sole regular shoes. It was very difficult to walk in these because the wooden sole had no flexibility, it didn't bend, as would a normal leather or rubber sole. As a consequence, I was constantly suffering from bruises on my ankles, which developed from the friction between my skin and the shoe. These sores never healed because of the lack of vitamins in my daily diet. I had their marks for years after the war.

One of the miracles, the cause of which I still don't comprehend, was that I stayed healthy. The clothing, including the coat for winter, was so thin that it couldn't provide any adequate protection from the fall and winter cold of Upper Silesia where Jaworznow was located. Still, I don't remember having the flu there or even catching an ordinary cold. I had those sores on my ankles, as I mentioned, and some diarrhea from time to time, but nothing else. I was in good health, without even a toothache, which I had plenty of later in life.

Like everyone else, I was starving all the time. There were two favorite subjects of discussion among the *Häftlings*: food and returning home. We talked about the various kinds of food that we used to eat at home. Similarly, we discussed how our return home would be organized. I fantasized with the friends I made in Jaworznow that there would be special trains to take us back to Hungary, each to his own town or village. The trains would leave from

Birkenau, just the way we were brought there, but the other way around. It was a childish fantasy, which might have resulted from listening to the non-stop rumors that constantly circulated in the camp. Maybe those rumors had some rational basis after all. In the summer of 1944, there was a temporary change in Horthy's policy in Hungary. Horthy dismissed the Stojay Government nominated after the German takeover of March 19 and named a new government headed by General Lakatos with a mandate to negotiate with the Soviet Union about the terms of Hungary's surrender.

The Germans torpedoed such a turn of events by kidnapping Horthy's son, who was the motor force behind the anti-Nazi efforts, deposing Horthy and putting Szalasi, the boss of the Hungarian Nyilas (Arrow Cross) Nazi Party, in power.

So all the rumors of things about to get better in Jaworznow were empty and all the speculation about going home soon evaporated.

I remember another rumor. This one had to do with the supposed death of Göring, Hitler's Deputy. Someone, somewhere, saw a newspaper with Göring's name printed on the front page inside a black rectangle. This could only mean that the man had died. It wasn't true, of course.

Looking back, however, this "news item" came to our attention around the time, in July 1944, when the von Staufenberg assassination attempt against Hitler took place. Naturally, there was no connection at all between the two events since there was no news printed about the plot against Hitler at the time and there was no way we could have known anything about such a highly secret event. But, besides the rumors and the talk about food and cooking, my main activity had to do with getting my hands on additional nourishment and also finding a suitable work assignment, to be protected from the severe cold of the season now that winter was approaching.

There was some additional food to be had at the *Krankenbau*. I don't know for what reason, but there was a sort of gruel allocated to the people there. Almost every evening I went there to "scout" for some of this gruel. One of the doctors, an Italian Jew who diagnosed me as suffering from *Systematischer Hartz Schwachheit* (systematic heart feebleness), was helpful in getting this extra portion of food for me. I never found out whether I really had symptoms of the above malady or if this Italian Jewish doctor invented it to help me get extra food.

In conjunction with these benefits, there was also a very unpleasant incident in conjunction with my frequent visits to the *Krankenbau*. I already mentioned the name of Mr. Fried, the father of the unfortunate Jancsi Fried. Mr. Fried was a graduate engineer and lucky enough to have a permanent job in the concentration camp working as an engineer in the office which prepared the blueprints for the hated *Gleisbau*.

He had a friend, a doctor from Kolozsvár (Cluj), who was successful in arranging work for himself in the *Krankenbau*. One evening after work in the barrack, Mr. Fried asked me to take a half portion of bread to his doctor friend in the *Krankenbau* since I was supposed to go there anyhow.

Both Mr. Fried and this doctor from Kolozsvár were respected among the *Häftlings* because of their behavior and also because of the somewhat privileged status both enjoyed. For some reason, I didn't go that particular evening to the *Krankenbau* and therefore asked one of my friends who was going, to deliver the bread. This boy was two or three years older than me and, together with his brother, was with me in the same barrack. They came from one of the villages in the vicinity of Nyiregyháza and were Orthodox Jews. I remember the "ideological" arguments we used to have. They claimed that the reason we were in the concentration camp was because God was punishing us all since I and others like me weren't religious enough. I, on the other hand, no less stupidly, argued that Jews were hated because of the way Orthodox Jews like them dressed, serving as a catalyst for antisemitism. So I gave the bread to one of them who promised to deliver it to the *Krankenbau*. Apparently the doctor from Kolozsvár never got the bread.

The next day, Mr. Fried confronted me with the charge that his friend hadn't received the bread. I explained to him that this boy promised to deliver the bread but I wasn't sure that Mr. Fried believed me. The brothers averted their eyes and seemed uncomfortable when I demanded an explanation but weren't willing to talk to either Mr. Fried or the doctor. The brothers most probably kept the bread for themselves. I never spoke to them after that incident and felt very bad vis-à-vis Mr. Fried because he knew me from home. Although he was a very private person, he was among the few grown-ups with whom I had had any relationship at all in the concentration camp.

This incident is also typical of my personality. Why was I so naive as to trust this boy to deliver the bread? Wasn't I supposed to doubt him, a stranger to me, and not to entrust him with bread in the concentration camp where it was such a precious item? On the one hand, it is dangerous to trust people; on the other hand, most times in my life, trusting people paid off.

Unfortunately, Mr. Fried didn't survive. He died because of a grave misfortune.

When, in January 1945, we were marched off to the West in what has become known as a death march, Mr. Fried arranged somehow with his connections to be allowed to stay behind in the *Krankenbau*. The Germans didn't execute those *Häftlings* who were allowed to stay behind, but during the Red Army's battle for Jaworznow some bombs fell on the *Krankenbau* and a number of *Häftlings* there were killed. Mr. Fried was one of them. My friend Boengi had also stayed behind but he luckily survived the attack.

◆

Let's go back to the daily routine in the concentration camp. In the evening, every evening, *Blocksperre* was announced. Everybody had to return to his barrack and not leave until morning. It was forbidden to go to the latrine during the night even though it was close to the barrack, but out of bounds during *Blocksperre*. A big tin was placed adjacent to the barrack door to be used only for pissing during the night. Since most of our food was liquid we had to get up a number of times during the night to use the tin.

I slept on the upper deck of my bunk, which was advantageous for a number of reasons, but was a nuisance when I had to climb up and down a number of times during the night. Still, I was young and had no problem in falling asleep right away after I returned to my bunk, no matter how many times during the night I woke up. However, nowadays, I know from personal experience that grown-ups don't always fall asleep as readily as children and realize that, from this aspect at least, it was easier for me as a child to survive in the concentration camp than it was for them. I recall that sometimes when my loneliness and general miserable situation got the upper hand, I tried to find a quiet place to cry and to sing to myself *Hatikvah*, the Zionist anthem.

At the end of the summer of 1944, something happened which more than anything else underlined the depth of my ignorance and how I didn't grasp the reality of our situation in the jaws of the SS. However, I wasn't the only one who didn't thoroughly understand the evil of the Nazi system of which we were the suffering objects.

One day in late September or early October, we were notified that a special SS commission would be coming to our camp. The task of this commission, or so we were told, was to choose *Häftlings* in bad physical shape who, because of the goodness of the Germans, would be eligible for rest and better nourishment. The lucky ones chosen would temporarily be transferred to a sanitarium to receive treatment and returned to Jaworznow after their physical condition had improved.

The truth behind this typical Nazi lie was that the SS were about to select the weak and sick for transport to Birkenau to be gassed and cremated. These were the preparations for the infamous October 1944 Selections when tens of thousands of *Häftlings* who were no longer fit to work were murdered.

Of course, I didn't know anything about what the SS were really up to. I have read recently in one of Primo Levy's books that he was incarcerated at the same time in Buna, a concentration camp adjacent to Auschwitz, and there the story circulated by the SS was that the weak would be taken to the Jaworznow "sanitarium" for rest and special nourishment.

So the day came and the SS selection commission arrived in Jaworznow. There was a special *Appel* and all the *Häftlings* were lined up in front of their barracks. An announcement was made that all those who thought they were weak and needed a rest were eligible for transfer to the sanitarium and should step forward. I stepped forward. Again I have to emphasize that I wasn't the only one who unwittingly volunteered to be murdered, which was the only consequence of stepping forward. Still, there *was* a certain logic in volunteering for what we believed was transportation to a place where we could rest and recuperate. There *was* after all a *Krankenbau* in our camp to treat *Häftlings* who had some minor ailment. The Germans *did* have an interest in our fitness for work to serve their purposes. Didn't they? I don't know. The more I think about it now, many years after the war, the less I understand Nazi logic.

However, most people convince themselves of what they want to believe. Therefore, it is no wonder that a number of *Häftlings* did step forward of their own free will at that fateful *Appel*. Additional *Häftlings*, besides those who volunteered, were pointed out by the *Blockältester* and ordered to step forward as well.

All who stepped forward were marched off to the Krankenbau where the selection process was taking place. We formed a single line. I took my place in the line, which moved slowly forward. At the head of the line were the

SS officers in charge of the selection, deciding the fate of each "sanitarium" candidate. However, several meters along the line, before each one reached the SS officers, stood the *Häftling* I mentioned before, the chief medical doctor of the camp. He was a German non-Jewish Communist prisoner.

The job of the *Häftling* doctor was to make a "pre-selection". He was to ensure that the SS officers' time was not wasted and that only really weak and sick *Häftlings* got to the SS. It is also possible that it was the *Häftling* doctor's idea to make this pre-selection in order to allow him to save the lives of some of those in line.

Anyhow, when my turn came to be confronted with the *Häftling* doctor he looked at me and ordered that I return at once to my barrack. In his view I was still fit to work and not be sent to my death. However, my mind registered his decision in a different way. It was as if I was being robbed of my chance to rest and eat better in the sanitarium, for a while at least, and I was angry. I decided that I wouldn't allow this chance for a rest to be denied because of this doctor's mood.

Instead of returning to my barrack as ordered, I joined the end of the line again and waited patiently for my turn to be chosen for the sanitarium. I was hoping that the *Häftling* doctor wouldn't remember me because there were so many others passing by him in the line. But to my great fortune he *did* remember me. When again, it was my turn, he recognized me and became angry. He, for sure, was aware of the *real* purpose of this selection process. He most probably wanted to save the life of this foolish child, and I was making it difficult for him. He shouted at me to get lost or else he would see to it that I was severely punished. So I had no choice but to resign myself to my fate and "bad luck" and return to the barrack.

All the *Häftlings* who were selected to go to the "sanitarium" were immediately segregated and put in a special barrack, which no one else was allowed to approach even from a distance. Slowly rumors were starting to circulate about the real fate awaiting those unfortunate men. After a couple of days, they were transported to an unknown destination. As the world found out after the war, they were all promptly gassed and cremated in Birkenau.

◆

Summer was over and it was starting to turn cold. I knew it was imperative to find work somewhere inside a workshop to be protected from the weather. The clerks, who were all *Häftlings*, had great influence in all aspects of life in the concentration camp. They were a very cohesive bunch of men. Most, if not all, of them were non-Jewish Czechs.

Somehow, through the Italian Jewish doctor I mentioned above, I found a way to approach one of these clerks. I begged him to try to arrange for me to work in the blacksmith shop at the power station. I had no training of course as a blacksmith or any other trade. This Czech clerk took pity on me and talked to the *Kapo* in charge of the blacksmiths. This *Kapo* originated from one of the villages of Transylvania and must have arrived in Jaworznow at the same time as my transport, at the beginning of June 1944. He was a shrewd and strong man and a blacksmith himself. So he worked himself up to become a *Kapo*. Maybe he was somehow under obligation to the clerk who wanted to help me and who, in turn, wanted to do the Italian doctor a favor. I suppose all those privileged *Häftlings* were doing favors to each other just the way the Mafia is said to operate. I really didn't know how exactly it came about, and didn't care, but I ended up working in the blacksmith shop just as the cold weather started.

Once again, my life was saved by a miracle. With only the thin clothing I have already described covering our bodies, it would have been impossible to survive for long if one had had to work outside for ten hours a day. Those *Häftlings* who were obliged to work outside in the freezing weather dropped like flies. Even the daily march to the power plant, which took something like twenty minutes each way, was terrible. But in the workshop it was O.K. There was a small stove with a fire, heating the place most of the time. To be truthful, I didn't do much work there. After all, I wasn't a blacksmith. I was given simple tasks to perform like polishing the various finished tools that the blacksmiths were producing. In addition to the *Kapo*, there was a Polish non-*Häftling* civilian who was directing the work. Whenever the SS inspector arrived, which was quite often I suppose because of the heat in the shop, I made myself look very busy and very professional; I doubt I fooled the others, but I definitely made an effort.

This *Kapo*, as I have mentioned, was a big and very noisy person. He was naturally feared by the *Häftlings* working for him but also respected because of his seeming fairness and folksiness. His *Pipel* was also working in the blacksmith shop and behaved very rudely trying to demonstrate to everyone that he was also a boss of some sort. I have explained above that a *Pipel* was a servant as well as a sexual object to his benefactor, in his case, the shop *Kapo*.

One morning, the *Kapo* yelled out for everyone to hear that he, the *Kapo*, had caught his *Pipel* red-handed during the night "fucking" somebody else. All this sounded a little mysterious to me because, as I mentioned, the real function of a *Pipel* wasn't very clear to me, but still, I think I did appreciate some of what this scene was all about. Anyhow, the *Kapo* started to strike his *Pipel* repeatedly in front of us. The wretched boy was crying, pleading to be forgiven while kissing the hands of the *Kapo* and promising him that such "mischief" would never occur again. I am not sure if we felt sorry for the boy. Anyhow, he never tried to boss us around after that incident.

The weather became colder and colder and my main concern was to keep warm, "organize" for myself as much food as possible, i.e. to stay alive. It was as if I had resigned myself to my fate as a *Häftling* and didn't have any idea what was going on in the world outside the concentration camp.

Then Christmas came and we, for the first time in the camp, found meat in our daily soup portion. In addition, we even got a real day off from work. My stomach was unaccustomed to such heavy food and I promptly got diarrhea. But I thought it worthwhile and would gladly have repeated eating meat once again, but it was of course only a dream.

After Christmas, everything returned to the daily toil already described.

DEATH MARCH

Then suddenly, all this routine was interrupted. One evening in mid-January while returning from work, we heard the unbelievable news. We were going to leave—the camp was going to be abandoned. As mentioned before, we, more precisely, I, didn't have the foggiest idea about the state of the war, either on the western or the eastern front. In the west, the Americans and British had already landed in June 1944 and by now Paris and, indeed, the whole of France was liberated. I also didn't know that the Red Army had occupied my hometown Nyiregyháza in November 1944 and that the siege of Budapest had started. In January 1945, the Red Army commenced its 1945 Winter Offensive in Poland as well, and was advancing on all fronts including in the direction of Jaworznow.

So we were told that, for some reason or other, we were going to be transferred to another concentration camp. We were to march to a nearby railroad station and be transported in train wagons to our new camp. After that announcement, there was a slight breakdown of discipline in the evening and the food store was looted.

I had a friend who was two years older than me but he was such a shy person that I was the "senior" in our relationship. He came from a small village near Nyiregyháza called Tiszaeszlár, which was the scene of the infamous blood libel that had taken place in 1882. In that blood libel, the Jews of Tiszaeszlár were accused of having murdered a young girl by the name of Eszter Solymosi and had used her blood to bake *Matzas* for Passover. The accusers took into custody one Móric Scharf, a pale Jewish lad, and forcefully convinced him to testify that he had witnessed the murder ritual with his own two eyes. Fifteen Jews were charged with the crime.

The trial took place in the courthouse of Nyiregyháza and a famous Hungarian non-Jewish lawyer by the name of Károly Eötvös conducted the defense. He succeeded in proving the innocence of the Jews accused of slaughtering the girl. It was a big trial, which aroused public opinion throughout Europe and so the name of Tiszaeszlár became famous, or more correctly, infamous.

So when the looting of food started in the camp, I, together with this boy from Tiszaeszlár, joined the crowd; we were able to place our hands on a large package of margarine, which we equally sliced up between the two of us. As it turned out, this piece of margarine was to be my only food for the next five days. I ate it all without even a grain of bread, and in consequence, again got an acute attack of diarrhea.

The time came to leave the camp. There was an *Appel* to make sure no one escaped this ordeal. There were some *Häftlings* missing from our barrack who tried to hide inside. They must have figured out for themselves the reason behind abandoning the concentration camp or maybe had some source of information about the situation outside and therefore figured that it would be best to stay behind. Some of those hiding in the barrack were discovered. I have no way of knowing whether there were others who were not found and thus stayed behind.

There were other *Häftlings* who were somehow lucky to be accepted into the Krankenbau and didn't leave with us. I discovered after my liberation, that in the battle between the Soviet Army and the Germans for Jaworznow, the concentration camp was bombarded and several *Häftlings* who were still in the Krankenbau were hit.

It was impossible for normal human beings to get to the bottom of Nazi logic. Take for instance the evacuation of our camp. The SS must have already known in the morning that the concentration camp would be abandoned in the evening. Still, they marched us off to work in the morning as they did every day and made sure that we put in an "honest" day of labor. For what? For what purpose? For whom?

We were erecting a power station. The Germans were about to abandon its site. So why put in an additional day's effort in building something that obviously wasn't going to be exploited for the good of the crumbling Third Reich? Remember, it was January 1945 and the Germans were retreating on all fronts. Even with the fierce resistance that the Germans put up in the West and in the East, everyone could see that they were losing the war.

As it turned out, the Germans never benefited from this power plant at all. In effect, we were building it for the benefit of the Polish state re-established after the fall of the Germans. I visited Jaworznow in 1989. The power plant was there, operating and supplying electricity to the citizens and industries of Jaworznow.

But in January 1945, the SS were taking us with them in their retreat. The camp gate, which was near our barrack, was opened. As a matter of fact, this was the same gate the trucks had entered in the spring of 1944 when we were first brought to the Jaworznow concentration camp. This time, however, there were no trucks; we had to march by foot. We were told that we would be transported by train, so we were thinking that this was going to be a short march, just until we got to the train wagons. We understood, of course, that we would travel in the same type of wagons that had delivered us to Birkenau. But there wasn't going to be any sort of train transportation for us. We were to march on and on by foot.

Leaving Jaworznow, we were approximately 3,000 *Häftlings*. After four days, when we arrived at the concentration camp of Blechhammer, this number had been reduced to around 300—a real death march.

It was terribly cold. As I have described above, our clothing was very meager. Three thin layers of cover between the body and the freezing outside temperature. The only supplementary items that an ordinary *Häftling* like me could lay his hands on were pieces of paper torn from the back of a sack of cement. This paper was carefully inserted between the shirt and the jacket and served as additional protection.

One of the biggest problems was our feet. I had wooden-soled shoes, very difficult to march in even for short distances because of the lack of flexibility in the sole. Now we were marching and marching. As it turned out it was a march of four whole days with very little rest. During those four days, we rested only twice. First, for a few hours in a concentration camp located not far from Sosnowiec after first marching a full day and then after the third day when we stopped for several hours during the night and spent it in some sort of large structure. During those four days we were given no food at all. There was only snow to quench our thirst.

Marching under such conditions was especially terrible because of a mathematical law dealing with "a column's progression" that regulates the movement of a long line of marching people. During a march, there is a time when one stands still. Then, this phase is followed by slow walking, which immediately turns into running. This mathematical law is demonstrated each time a line of cars stops at a red traffic light and then starts to move as the light changes to green. Everyone driving a car knows that if one is, let's say, in the fifth or sixth car he doesn't move right away. It takes a few seconds after the first car starts to move before the fifth or sixth car can move as well. This delay is then compensated by increasing speed as the first cars gain distance in front. It is no big problem when you are driving a car, but it is terrible when you are on foot in a long line of marchers and one is number thirty or forty in the row. One first waits a lot and then one runs a lot.

It is very tiring during the running phase. On the other hand, one is freezing during the standing phase because the body generates less heat standing than walking or running. It was, therefore, best to be at the head of the marching column where the changes in the marchers' velocity were minimal.

Naturally, the strongest *Häftlings* who were able to keep up with the rate of marching were at the head of the column. The weaker ones couldn't keep up with the speed required. So by the law of cybernetics, a positive feedback situation developed. Those *Häftlings* who were already weak and thus couldn't keep up with the pace at the front of the line, found themselves at the back. There, they tired even more and became even weaker because of the phenomenon of a "column's progression". Those *Häftlings* who were too exhausted to march on, and therefore gradually regressed to the back, eventually gave up walking and were instantly shot by the SS guards. This fact explains why only one tenth of the *Häftlings* survived the death march.

I was terribly tired, hungry and cold. My feet, especially, were freezing. At one point during the march, I found myself beside Mr. Pogány. I think this was his name but I am not a hundred percent certain. The Pogány family in Nyiregyháza lived in our neighborhood. He was a respected and important executive of MAV, the Hungarian Railroad Company. I often saw him walking to the railroad station in his shining uniform and gold-laced cap. I don't remember whether in Jaworznow concentration camp we ever had an occasion to speak to each other. He must have been in a different barrack. Mr. Pogány was a tall, lean man in his late forties, I think. He had only one child, a son. The son was not one of my friends because he was several years younger. Obviously and unfortunately, he must have been among those children who were immediately gassed and cremated upon arrival in Birkenau.

Mr. Pogány didn't realize or didn't want to accept the possibility that his son was long dead. So, walking alongside him, he started to talk to me. He told me that he was very weak and most probably wouldn't make it. Therefore, he wanted to ask me a favor. I should promise him that if and when I am liberated and return home to Nyiregyháza I should look up his son and tell him where some of their money and jewelry were hidden. Pogány went on explaining to me what was hidden and where it was hidden. To be truthful, I don't think that I fully digested that information. I wasn't much interested. Still I pretended to listen. Why? Because Pogány promised to share with me a piece of bread he had with him, if I just listened.

In the dynamics of the march we then drifted away from each other and I don't recall that I was ever given that piece of bread. I never saw Mr. Pogány again. Most probably he was shot like all the others who had no strength to go on. I didn't, of course, meet his son back in Nyiregyháza. No one returned from the Pogány family. Most probably the treasure is still where Mr. Pogány put it before deportation.

As the days and hours passed during the march, more and more shots were heard. We all knew what it signified—an additional unfortunate *Häftling* had given up and was murdered by the guards. One of the terrible stories I was told later on by Pista Lipkovits, my friend and cousin who survived the march, was related to his father. The father was so tired that he couldn't go on and asked Pista to let him sit down and lean against a tree. Pista did as he requested and then had to march on, otherwise he would have been shot as well. As he walked away from his father, Pista heard the shot. He couldn't bring himself to turn his head and see his father dead.

Pista was one of my good friends in Nyiregyháza who had introduced me to Zionism when I joined the *Hashomer Hatzair* youth movement. He was then called Nachman and wanted to be a carpenter in *Eretz Yisrael*. His older brother, Gyori, whom Pista admired, was also a Zionist. Gyori was shot in 1944 while trying to escape from a deportation transport on its way to Auschwitz.

Pista was one of the founding members of Kibbutz Gaaton where he now lives. In addition to his regular job in the kibbutz, he is also an artist and has exhibited his works several times over the years. Pista is married to a wonderful woman by the name of Bat Ami who was born in Argentina. They have three daughters and a son and I don't know how many grandchildren. Pista is now called Dov Gonen.

◆

On the fourth day of the march, I became so tired that I decided to step out of the marching column to be shot and be done with it. I actually stepped out of the column. To my unbelievable luck, one of the guards walking some meters behind me apparently heard me speaking Hungarian and understood the language. Anyhow, he pushed me back into the column and said to me in Hungarian, "Son, I am not like the others. I don't want to shoot you." So I survived for another couple of hours. Later on, I again felt that I had no strength left to continue. As I mentioned above, there are instances in a marching column when first you don't move and then you have to run. When we stopped, I sat down on the ground utterly exhausted. I decided not to get up when the column started to move again. However, someone starting to march bumped into me, so I got up and began to walk again. This time, however, I was so utterly exhausted that I couldn't even keep my trousers up. Somewhere during the march I had lost the metal wire that served as a belt and my pants were slipping off my hips. I had to grab the pants with my hands to keep them in place. This effort added to the energy I had to exert. Maybe it sounds stupid now in the realm of normal life, how something like a missing belt can be so critical to one's endurance. But after four days of cold, no nourishment and utter exhaustion, every small difficulty became critical.

By the end of the fourth day I felt that I really couldn't go on. Then suddenly, two young men from Nyiregyháza, Pista Lipkovits's neighbors, came to my rescue. I don't know how, but apparently they noticed my condition and had enough strength and humanity left in them to come and help me. They grabbed my arms, one on each side and thus supported me as we marched on.

How differently people are judged under various circumstances is illustrated by the fact that when I told Pista many years later how his neighbors had saved my life, he was astonished. He told me that on returning to Nyiregyháza in the winter of 1945 he had had an unpleasant experience with the same two men relating to the Lipkovits family's property.

CHAPTER 3

THE LONG ROAD "HOME"

FIRST TASTE OF FREEDOM

Half an hour or so later, our marching column, or what was left of it, was led into a concentration camp located in a wooded area. We had arrived in Blechhammer. Suddenly there were no guards to be seen. A murmur went through the crowd. The SS are gone. We are free. It was unbelievable news. Two Jaworznow *Blockältesters*, Vogel was one of them, climbed onto some sort of a rostrum, and addressing the crowd, urged us to keep calm. After that, we quickly dispersed to find a place to sleep. Pista Lipkovits and I found ourselves together. We located a bunk and some blankets in one barrack. We were in shock after everything we had gone through—he had lost his father; we were both exhausted but alive and now this incredible discovery that the SS were gone.

We experienced an intense emotional upheaval. I think it can only be compared to the feelings of an intensely sick person on the verge of death when informed by his doctor that it was all a big mistake and he would recover from his malady. We kissed, embraced and swore to each other that from then on we would be like brothers, keeping together and protecting each other. We then fell into a deep and long sleep. I don't know how many hours we had been sleeping when we awoke to the noise of gunshots and the smell of smoke in our nostrils. We quickly got off the bunk. Outside the barrack, three or four meters from where we were standing was a row of some eleven SS soldiers. The SS were shooting at people in the barrack next to us.

Luckily the soldiers were with their backs to us, so we couldn't be seen. Pista and I didn't lose a moment. We slipped out of the barrack where we had been sleeping. We ran in the opposite direction to the shooting, desperately looking for a place to hide.

We located a very small shack with some food in it. Unbelievable—we had found a place to hide and food. The food was sour cabbage, only sour cabbage, and lots of sour cabbage. We hadn't eaten for days and we were famished. I ate a lot of the sour cabbage, drinking its juice as well. I think Pista did the same. I was to spend many days and nights during the following week at the latrine with a severe attack of diarrhea.

We spent several hours in this shack. When it was getting dark and we heard no more shots, we gathered sufficient courage to leave and to try to find a place to sleep. The camp's streets were deserted, neither a *Häftling* nor a SS guard was to be seen.

We walked for a while and finally found ourselves in the area where the Krankenbau barracks were located. In one of these barracks there was a small room with some *Häftlings* in a few beds. We decided to settle in there and made one of the empty bunks our home. This place was to be our base for several days to come. We went to sleep hungry and awoke the next morning even hungrier. We desperately had to find some food.

Roaming the streets, we came upon a small crowd pushing and shouting around a dead horse. In charge of carving up the horse was a relatively healthy looking man, in his forties, wearing *Häftling* clothing. He was cutting it up and distributing horsemeat to whoever was able to get near enough to the action. Pista and I weren't energetic enough and didn't get any of the red meat but only the horse's liver. We took the liver and returned to our barrack where there was a stove and fire. We were so hungry, however, that we didn't have the patience to wait for the liver to properly roast. We ate our barely edible portions half raw. Even though we were starving, the taste of the liver was terrible. But we quickly devoured it to the last bite.

◆

The person cutting up the horse was Jenő Rubinstein—this was the first but not the last time I would bump into him. Of course, there in Blechhammer, I didn't know his name or who he was.

I met Jenő the second time in March 1948 in Paris, France. I was on my way to *Eretz Yisrael*. My group was in Marseilles waiting for our turn to sail. I made contact with my Aunt Jolan in Paris. She was the widow of my uncle Miksa Sichermann who had passed away in Paris in 1943.

Jolan had found out from correspondence with my Aunt Margit in Wilkes-Barre, Pennsylvania, that I had survived the war. Aunt Margit had searched for any survivors of the Sichermann family. That's how she found out about me being the sole survivor of my family. This information was relayed by Margit to Jolan. Jolan sent a letter to the UNRRA (United Nations Relief and Rehabilitation Administration) to locate me and they forwarded it to me. By the time UNRRA found me we were already in Marseilles. I wrote to her right away and Jolan sent me money in a letter in which she invited me to come to Paris. Through additional correspondence, we settled the date, the train station and the time I would arrive.

Jolan and the other members of the family were waiting for me on time at the station but somehow we missed each other and I took a tram to Jolan's home at 15 Rue de la Clef. As it turned out, I got there before Jolan and other members of the family who were still looking for me at the station.

I rang the bell and a man with his shirtsleeves rolled up opened the door. I introduced myself and looked at his left arm. There was a *Häftling* number tattooed there. I asked him in which concentration camp he was and where he was liberated. "The last concentration camp I was in was Blechhammer and I was also liberated there," the man said. "I was also liberated in Blechhammer," I replied.

I took a closer look at him. There was something familiar about this man. Yes, you've guessed it right. Jenő Rubinstein was the man who had truncated and distributed the flesh of the horse in January 1945, three years before. I reminded him of the event which he remembered well. He also seemed to recollect two young boys who were trying to push forward for their portion of the horse.

Jenő Rubinstein had married my Aunt Jolan after the war upon returning to Paris from Blechhammer. His first wife unfortunately perished like so many others in one of the Nazi death camps.

As Jenő told me later, he was born in a small village in South Transylvania. As a young man he had gone to live in France. After the war he was left a widower with three grown-up children, two daughters and a son who was the youngest. We immediately found a common language between the two of us. After that encounter in March 1948, we became good friends for many years to come. We met several times in Paris and in Israel and enjoyed being together each and every time. Aunt Jolan died before Jenő and he followed her sometime in the 1980s. He must have been over 90 years old when he passed away. I liked him a lot.

ENCOUNTERING SOVIET TROOPS

But back in Blechhammer the Soviet Army was fast approaching and still the SS didn't give up. They wanted the former *Häftlings*, like us, who felt that they were already free, to return to their former *Häftling* status. Only they knew why it was so important for them, less than four months before the total collapse of the thousand-year Reich. Although, I doubt that they themselves really understood why it was so important for them to drag the *Häftlings* all the way to Germany. One of my former schoolmates from Nyiregyháza, Laci Kun, whose name I have already mentioned, was rounded up with others in Blechhammer and hauled off to the West—he was liberated only in May 1945 in the concentration camp of Mauthausen.

One night while I was sitting on the latrine outside the barrack because of my sauerkraut diarrhea, I noticed SS soldiers in white ski uniforms looking for *Häftlings*. Luckily, they couldn't see me because it was dark where I was sitting, but I saw them.

Then suddenly, the battle for Blechhammer and the region began. There was shooting, with Katyusha rockets and mortar shells exploding all around. A wounded man was brought into our barrack. In the evening, he was still alive in the bunk beneath ours but he died during the night. There were some doctors among the former *Häftlings* who were making daily rounds in the barracks but couldn't help much because of the lack of medicine and bandages. One of those doctors was Dr. Havas whom I knew from Nyiregyháza and also from Jaworznow. One day, when he visited our barrack he didn't recognize me; I was in such bad shape, even relative to my condition a week before in Jaworznow.

Then the first Soviets troops arrived in black uniforms and we greeted them enthusiastically. I quickly learned to say, *Zdrastvuti Tovarish,* which means, "Welcome Comrade", and repeated it all the time, to every soldier I met. They gave us bread, dark black bread. That's what they ate themselves. The Red Army didn't feed its fighters any luxuries. I think that arms and ammunition supplies had a much higher priority for them than the supply of food. Pista and I decided to go outside the camp to look for food. We found that besides the Blechhammer concentration camp, there were a number of other camps for various types of civilian workers that the Germans had enslaved. All those camps were vacant. There wasn't much food to be found there either. We did, however, locate some warm clothing. I was still wearing this clothing when I finally arrived in Nyiregyháza on Monday, March 5, 1945.

It was a wonderful, sunny, cold winter day in late January, and we were free. I distinctly recall the feeling. No longer forced to march to the German order of "*links, zwei, drei, vier; links, zwei, drei, vier*", "left, two, three, four; left, two, three, four". We were free to walk as fast or as slow as we wished. Nobody was there to order us around. The importance of freedom, of being a free person doing what one wants to do has been with me ever since. For me, the most important issues in one's life are to be alive and healthy and to live in a free and democratic society.

Up until today, I have been lucky to have spent my entire adult life under such circumstances. I have always lived in free, democratic and liberal societies, whether in Israel or in the U.S. I pray and hope that my children and grandchildren will also be able to enjoy such privileges their entire lives.

Now that the Red Army had arrived in Blechhammer, Pista and I assumed that they would soon organize proper transportation for us to return home to Hungary. It took us only a few days to awaken from this naive pipe dream. We realized that no one was going to organize any transportation; the Red Army still had a war to fight and the fate of the liberated *Häftlings* was the least of their concerns.

So one morning, it was snowing as I recall, we started out on our long walk back to Hungary. In the village nearby we got a lift in a horse-drawn cart for a while. We then had to walk and rest wherever we could find shelter from the cold. During our advance, we were joined by other former *Häftlings*. Maybe it was the other way around and we joined them. It really didn't matter. Finally we were five, all Jews—Pista and I, a Czech guy, another from Holland

and one from Poland. From the beginning, Pista seemed to remember something very bad about the Polish man from the death march, but later he came to the conclusion that he had misidentified him. The Polish Jew turned out to be the least disagreeable among the three. The Dutch Jew was the worst.

It didn't take us too long to arrive in Gliwice, which is a medium-sized town in Upper Silesia. We headed towards the *Komandatura*, the headquarters of the Red Army, to ask for help. The *Komandatura* was located in the largest hotel in town.

We found the place and were waiting for our turn to talk to someone in authority. It was then that I half noticed a person who was dressed in a *Häftling* outfit being led by a Russian soldier behind the hotel. Then we heard shooting from where this person disappeared with the soldier. In a little while the soldier returned alone. At the time, I didn't think much about it. I was too busy attending to our own business with the *Komandatura*. Several days later, however, under very different circumstances, I recalled this incident and it sent shivers through my bones. But I will come to that later.

Finally our turn came to talk with the officer in charge in the *Komandatura*. Our looks disclosed that we were ex-inmates of the Germans and we didn't have to justify ourselves in asking for help. We asked for food and some place to sleep. We were given an address and told to expel the Germans living there, take over the apartment and take whatever food, etc. we would find there. We were most likely directed to that particular address because the Soviets had a list of apartments that were occupied by Germans who had been transferred there after Germany occupied Poland in order to Germanize some areas. Upper Silesia was one of the regions that the Nazis wanted for Germans only.

We located the apartment and found a very frightened German family there. They had already moved from the better rooms before our arrival into a side room that might have belonged in the past to the domestic help. The Red Army must have ordered them to do so beforehand. The Germans wanted to appear very hospitable to us. They started to justify themselves right away by stating that they didn't know anything about any concentration camps, *Häftlings*, forced labor, etc. They claimed to have found out about these horrors only with the arrival of the Red Army. This was, of course, a very unbelievable tale. I distinctly recalled that during the "death march" of only a couple of weeks ago, while passing through these Upper Silesian towns, I saw people in the streets. They saw how ragged and miserable we were, barely dragging ourselves along. They knew very well who these people were. Besides, there were many concentration camps in this general area of Gliwice, Sosnowiec, etc. Civilian workers were employed for various jobs in the camps. They must have reported to their wives what they saw there. So there wasn't any other possibility but that the population was aware of the hell created by the SS all around their towns. Is it possible to imagine that the SS soldiers on their leave of absence, drunk or sober, didn't boast, complain or explain about the goings on inside those concentration camps? After all, we are talking about a period that lasted more than five years, from 1939 to 1945.

In addition to the SS, there were also civilians working at the various sites where *Häftlings* were engaged as slave labor. I don't have any doubt that the German civilian population everywhere in Germany and in the occupied territories knew, in general terms at least, most of what was going on inside the camps. In Upper Silesia, even the deaf and blind must have known.

CONFRONTING SOVIET RULE

Anyhow, the five of us moved into the apartment. There was some food, there were beds, a kitchen and even a piano in the dining room. My fingers were stiff, but I recall playing the *Fantasy in D Minor* by Mozart. Since we were just young boys, the three grown-ups in our group made us do all the house-work. As I mentioned, with the exception of the Polish Jew, the Czech and especially the Dutch Jew were not very nice to us. The Dutch and Czech didn't have any possibility to return to their countries yet because the war was still raging there. Therefore, these two weren't in any hurry to leave.

However, Pista and I didn't overly enjoy ourselves in their company. Since the areas we had to cross to get home to Nyiregyháza were already in the hands of the Red Army, there was no reason for us to stay on. One morning we decided that we had had enough of this life and left the apartment to carry on with our journey back to Hungary. I have no idea what became of the men we left behind; we never encountered them again.

Pista and I directed ourselves again to the *Komandatura*. There, we were lucky to meet a Jewish officer. With broken Yiddish, we explained to him that we were Hungarian Jews who had been interned in a Nazi concentration camp. Later, I learned to say in Polish, or what I thought was Polish, *ja idziem d'obozu* (I come from a concentration camp).

We asked the Jewish Red Army officer to help us get home to Hungary. He seemed to know about the fate of the Jews under Nazi rule. He was friendly to us, obviously trying to help. He sent us to a school building, which was used by the Red Army as its lodging. According to this Jewish officer, some trucks were to be leaving the next morning for the southeast, which was our general direction as well, and we were welcome to hitch a ride with them.

We found the place from where the trucks were to leave and soon enough we were sitting in the company of the Russian soldiers there, most of them young boys. We were all eating and drinking and singing together. They were friendly to us and it was a very enjoyable evening. They confirmed that the next morning there would be trucks leaving in our direction and that they would let us travel with them. Before falling asleep, all of us sleeping on the floor in the same place where we ate and sang, we made them promise to wake us early in the morning to ensure that we wouldn't miss the trucks.

The heavy eating and the vodka we drank ensured that we slept well, so well in fact that when Pista and I awoke next day it was already late morning.

We looked around but there was nobody there. The room was empty. We looked out into the yard where the trucks were supposed to be but the yard was also completely empty. It was quiet, with no sound to be heard. Obviously, everyone had left. But because of our Hungarian education which wasn't completely shattered, even in the concentration camp, we were convinced that if the Russians, who at that time were still like gods in our eyes, told us that there would be trucks, then there should be trucks arriving even if they were a little late. We waited and waited. Nothing happened. No trucks. No nothing. Then suddenly there was a noise. Someone was running up the stairs. The door opened and a Russian soldier illuminated the room with an electric torch. He was obviously searching for something. Then he left and ran up the stairs. We heard him opening and shutting doors and then after a minute or two he returned. He was asking us something. Relying only on our less than minimal Russian knowledge, we realized that he was looking for someone. Now again, our Hungarian education came to our "rescue". Our subconscious thoughts went something like this, "If the Russians (gods) promised that we will travel with them in their trucks then obviously this soldier was sent to fetch us and is about to take us to the trucks." Pointing at ourselves, we volunteered to be the people he was looking for.

We followed him into the street, but were a little astonished to see that he was taking us in the direction of the *Komandatura*. On our way there, I saw the Russian Jewish officer of the day before. He seemed to be amazed to see us again but we didn't exchange any words. In fast steps, we were led by the Russian soldier who had found us. It was becoming more and more obvious that we were on our way to the *Komandatura*. The unfriendly behavior of the soldier accompanying us was less and less to our liking. We arrived at the *Komandatura* and were led straight to a woman officer. She started to interrogate us. She spoke broken German. "Who are you, where do you come from," she wanted to know. "We are Hungarian Jewish children just liberated by the Red Army from a Nazi concentration camp waiting for the trucks to take us home," we told her in German.

"That is not what I am asking you," she retorted. "I want to know where you are from in Germany." It was clear that she didn't speak German very well and didn't understand or didn't want to understand us. After several minutes of this futile exchange between the deaf and mute, she ordered us to be taken into custody. We were prisoners. We were led to the basement. A door was opened and we were pushed into a cell.

But we were not alone. The cell was full of men. Some in German *Wehrmacht* uniforms, some in SS uniforms, some civilians. They were all Germans. Now we understood what had happened. The Russian soldier who brought us to the *Komandatura* had been sent to the barracks to fetch some suspicious characters who must have been caught by the Red Army before. The Russians mistook us for these men. We foolishly helped them in this misidentification when we "volunteered" to be led by the soldier to the *Komandatura*. When we figured out all this we started to cry. The other prisoners treated us as one of their own. They were asking us questions about whom we were and why the Russians had arrested us. They also thought that we were like them, Germans, or at least sympathizers. We realized that we had maneuvered ourselves into this very dangerous situation. I suddenly remembered that the day we first arrived to Gliwice, I had seen this concentration camp-uniformed person being led behind the *Komandatura* and that shots had followed. Most certainly, an execution. "Have I escaped alive from the Nazis only to be shot by the liberating Red Army?" It was a frightening thought. I don't know how long we were in this situation in the cell silently weeping most of the time—maybe several hours, maybe less. Then unexpectedly the cell door opened.

Outside there was a group of maybe eleven Russians who appeared to be high-ranking officers. Most probably they came to decide about the fate of each prisoner. I noticed the female officer who sent us here. Then a ray of hope—in the midst of this group of Russian officers, I recognized the Jewish officer. I made a sign so he would notice us. He did notice and I saw that he recognized us. He pushed himself, from behind where he stood, to the front. "What are you doing here?" he whispered to us. He grabbed us both by the arm, pulled us out of the cell, and murmured-ordered, "Get out of here as fast as you can." He didn't have to say it twice. We immediately disappeared. We ran as fast as we could, from the basement, from the *Komandatura* building. An important lesson in my education, let's call it "de-Hungarization", was given to me. "Don't jump without thoroughly understanding what the jumping is all about."

We had been saved from a very dangerous situation. I don't know what happened to all the Germans who were with us in that cell and I don't care. But even assuming that Pista and I wouldn't have been executed as German spies or something, it was quite possible that the Russians would have deported us to Siberia as they did with so many people, Jews and gentiles alike, that they encountered during the war.

Some of those deported were thus innocent of any wrongdoing; they were just unlucky in being in the wrong place at the wrong time. One such man was Jamoy Holländer, whom I met in 1947 in Strüth, Germany, waiting for our turn for *Aliya Bet* (clandestine immigration) to *Eretz Yisrael*. Jamoy was a member of *Hashomer Hatzair* from childhood and was ardently pro-Communist and pro-Soviet. He was quite casually caught by the Russians on the street somewhere in Hungary. Jamoy had just been liberated by the Red Army and was returning from forced labor in the fascist Hungarian Army.

These facts didn't much matter to the Russians. First, they took him for what was called *troska roboti*, "a little work", and then for some unexplained reason they deported him to Siberia where he was lucky to be held for only two years and then sent home. Jamoy was born in a little town, which after the war was annexed by the Russians to the Soviet Union and therefore he had priority in repatriation. After Gliwice, the "godly" status of the Red Army, in my eyes, was shaken.

As time went by and I encountered more and more soldiers of the Red Army, my disillusionment grew. I was happy when, in January 1946, I saw the last of them in Budapest and later in Vienna. Nevertheless, I will forever remember with gratitude the fact that I was liberated by the Red Army. My life was saved by its soldiers. Also, there is no doubt in my mind that the defeat of the Nazi regime should mainly be attributed to the heroic fight of the Red Army and the resistance of the Soviet people.

Of course, under the circumstances of our recent arrest experience, we didn't even dream of trying to locate those trucks, which, if they ever existed, were supposed to have taken us towards our destination.

ON THE ROAD AGAIN

Leaving Gliwice, Pista and I headed east to Kraków. Under the conditions of those days in February 1945, it was easier for us to find food while in Upper Silesia. It had a large German population and under the occupation was considered to be part of Germany. Food supplies there were much more plentiful than in the areas of the so-called General Government as all the other parts of pre-1939 Poland were called. Gliwice, for instance, was in Upper Silesia. Kraków, under the Germans, was in the General Government.

In February 1945, regular food supply in all of Poland was still lacking. People had to manage from their reserves. German areas had reserves; Polish areas didn't. In addition, in February 1945, the Germans in Upper Silesia were terrified and it wasn't difficult as an ex-*Häftling* to induce them to share their food. The Germans were now occupied by the Red Army whereas the Poles had been "liberated" by them. The Poles had no food to share and also were not afraid to say "no" when asked.

In Kraków, therefore, we suffered terribly from hunger. Kraków is a beautiful city, which wasn't damaged much during the war. I visited the city twice in the 1990s, when I was able to appreciate its beauty. However, in February 1945, I didn't enjoy staying there, to say the least. After arriving in Kraków with Pista, we located the place where former Jewish *Häftlings* had been given temporary shelter. It was a building that had apparently belonged to the Jewish Community before the war. During all the years since, I thought that this house was located on ulica Druga (Druga Street), but when I visited Kraków in the 1990s I couldn't find it. In 1945, the building itself was in quite good basic condition but there weren't any beds, blankets, food or anything else there. Kraków had only recently been liberated, the war was still being waged and the city was still in chaos. The place was packed with people, mostly men—all ex-*Häftlings* in run-down physical and mental condition. Everyone was hungry. Everyone was searching for family survivors. I was constantly inquiring about my parents. I asked anyone who was willing to answer, whether they knew or had heard or had seen any sign of my father and mother. Nothing at all. I couldn't get any information about them. Were they alive or did they perish? Nobody had any information for me; nobody knew anything. Everybody was busy attending to his own problems.

During the night, Pista and I slept together on the floor. The toilet, such as it was, wasn't intended for so many people. It was clogged up and had flooded all over the floor. During the night, when people had to piss, they got up and relieved themselves in one of the vacant rooms. Everything stunk. Pista and I were so desperate that I remember us crying and telling each other that even the concentration camp was better than this. I am ashamed now for thinking this at the time, because freedom is one of the most supreme values. But then, in Kraków, we were desperate.

We had no money and there was no food for us. We were given nothing to eat at the place where we slept so the only way was to beg for food. I learned to say something like, "*Prosze pani trosko chleba albo objad*", which I thought meant in Polish, "Please sir/lady a little bread or lunch." Armed only with this sentence, we knocked on doors asking for something to eat. As I explained above, the citizens of Kraków also lacked so much that few people obliged. One exception was a lady, I think in her thirties, whose apartment was on the other side of the river. She was really nice and she took pity on me. I don't recall whether I went to her place with Pista or alone, but she gave me a decent lunch and even instructed me not to be ashamed and to return another day.

We stayed a few days in Kraków until I realized that I wouldn't find any information there about my parents. It was also becoming obvious that there wouldn't be any organized effort in the near future to transport us back to Hungary. We, therefore, decided to leave and continue our journey home on our own.

By that time, however, the relationship between Pista and I had deterio-rated a lot. Actually this was no wonder. We were cold, hungry and exhausted. There was nobody to help us. Remember, we were only a little over fourteen years old. Pista had seen his father murdered just a few days before and I was disappointed and aching at not having found any news about my own parents. One day, the two of us broke up. We didn't plan it in advance and it wasn't a voluntary parting either, but it happened. This is the way it was. After Kraków, we had found shelter in a freight train waiting for it to move to the south, when Russian soldiers boarded the train looking for people to be taken for "a little work". They took Pista and some others, but left me alone. A little later, the train started to move but Pista was still not back. We were both on our own.

I didn't encounter Pista any time later during my journey back to Nyiregyháza. The next time I met Pista was in Israel in May 1948. I, with my *Hashomer Hatzair* group, had just arrived at Kibbutz Yakum when I saw a familiar figure approaching through the fields. I couldn't believe my eyes. It was Pista. He had arrived earlier in Israel, had somehow found out where I was and had come to visit me. He stayed in Yakum with me for only a short time as he had to hitchhike in both directions, which wasn't that easy, even then. It was very touching of him to seek me out, although I learned to ap-preciate this gesture only much later on. As it turned out, and despite the fact that Pista had been taken from the wagon in Poland, he reached our hometown of Nyiregyháza before me. When I finally arrived in Nyiregyháza on March 5, 1945, he had already left for Budapest to join *Hashomer Hatzair* there. So, after the Russians removed Pista from the train for "a little work" in Poland, it took us more than three years to see each other again.

At the time that Pista was taken by the Russians, I joined a group of other Hungarian Jewish youth trying to return home. I remember passing through a small Polish town where we somehow heard about a local Jew who had returned. We found his address and went to his apartment. Seeing us, the man was obviously frightened. How was it that his "secret", that a Jew had returned to his hometown, was already out? He wasn't happy to see us at all. He must have known that the Poles didn't like their Jews alive and returning.

He demanded that we leave him alone and go. That's what we did—we left. At the time, I didn't completely understand his attitude but later, from my own personal experience, I realized that this Jew was justified in his anguish.

Now, of course, it is widely known that Poles also committed atrocities against Jews both during the war and, astonishingly, even after the liberation. I have personal experience with Poles and their deep-rooted antisemitic feelings.

With this little group of Hungarian Jewish youth, we slowly proceeded toward the south in the direction of Krosno and found ourselves in a small village looking for lodging. Someone on the street directed us to the office of the village council and there each of us was directed to stay in the home of a Polish family. There were three or four youngsters in our small group and each was directed to a different house.

My host was a single Polish man. He lived in a small house with pictures of Christian saints decorating his walls. He was a nice and kind person. At this stage of my wanderings in Poland, I already knew that it was more advisable to present myself as just Hungarian rather than a Hungarian Jew. So I told my host that I was a Hungarian youth on my way home from a forced labor camp. I spoke the Polish language sufficiently to converse with the man. I remember myself repeating to him again and again that "Polski, Węgrski jedno", "Poles, Hungarians one". It was clear that he liked what I was saying about Polish-Hungarian friendship. In fact, just before September 1939 and the German occupation of Poland, there was a strong official movement backed by the Hungarian government advocating Hungarian-Polish friendship with the slogan of "A Common Hungarian-Polish Border".

Apparently, there was a similar movement in Poland advocating Polish-Hungarian friendship. In 1939, before the German invasion, the Poles could have used all the friends they could get. After the German occupation and dissolution of the Czech-Slovak Republic, the Hungarians, of course, wanted the territory of the Slovak "state" that was sandwiched between Hungary and Poland, and thus the call for a common Hungarian-Polish border. The Poles, of course, were looking for international support to survive. It didn't help them a lot.

By that time, my frostbitten right foot was in terrible shape. The right toe was putrid, full of pus and gave off a strong stench. My host, the Pole, this kind-hearted and good man, removed the paper bandage my foot was wrapped in, washed my foot, put some ointment on and wrapped it in a proper bandage. I stayed with him for a couple of days. He shared with me what meager food he had.

Then came the shock.

He was naive enough to believe my story that I was merely Hungarian and not a Hungarian Jew. One late afternoon, he took me to the window and showed me a small forest, some hundred meters from the house. He said to me, "Look at that forest, do you see it well?" I replied, "Yes, I see it well." Then he said full of emotion, "This is the place where we finished off our Jews." Just imagine what went through my mind at that moment. I was terrified; I was frightened. I wanted to leave the house immediately. I hardly slept during that night, waiting for the morning to escape. Our little group was scheduled to be on its way next morning anyhow.

Next morning we met at the village square. Each of us was accompanied by his host. I noticed the other Poles and my host whispering to each other. I told the others to run from the place as fast as possible. I conjectured from the whispering of the Poles that the others, besides my host, knew that we were Jewish. My host who was misled to believe that I wasn't Jewish had confided to me either the village secret of murdering the Jews or was just boasting a figment of his imagination. I couldn't know the truth. In any case it was dangerous for us to stay there a moment longer. We ran. Later, I explained to my friends what had happened. It was as I imagined. None of them had hidden the fact from his host that he was Jewish. To be truthful, despite this information about being Jewish, none of the others in my group complained about having been treated badly.

This story about my Polish host made me think about antisemitism in Poland. My host behaved like a good, kind person. He was compassionate to a complete stranger whom he believed to be a Hungarian friend, representative of Polish-Hungarian friendship. Then, as an important act of "brotherhood", he disclosed his deeply held secret about the killing of "their" Jews.

I now, however, think that maybe it was something else. It is possible that my host's motives were different. Perhaps he had guessed all along that I was Jewish; I never actually told him that I wasn't, I just didn't tell him that I was. He might have just been pulling my leg or testing me with this terrible story. Who knows? Even this alternative version doesn't necessarily alter my observation about the antisemitism of even a basically kind and compassionate Polish peasant.

Later in the 1990s, when I lived for a while in the U.S., I visited Poland several times. I was part of the American side of an American-Polish joint venture. I observed the Poles in Warsaw. They were so different in appearance from Jews. Jews generally have a dark complexion. The average Pole is fair looking. The facial expression is also very different.

Before the war, when there were so many Jews living in Warsaw, it must have been fairly obvious who was Jewish and who wasn't. What does this mean? Not much! Does it, in any way justify or even explain the antisemitism of the average Pole? Not at all!

The obvious physical difference between Poles and Jews is an observation with not much meaning. For me, the roots of the harsh Polish antisemitism must be sought in the ardent Catholic religiosity of the Poles. I will never forget an episode in Claude Lanzmann's film, *Shoah*. In one of the villages similar to the one where I had the horrid experience just described, Lanzmann was interviewing people on a Sunday morning as they were leaving church. Lanzmann initiated a conversation about the fate of the Jews of their village. One Pole, quite well dressed, it was Sunday after all, recollected what he had heard about the events at the critical moment when the Jews were assembled in the village square and about to be led away. "The rabbi addressed the Jews," this Pole recounted. "The rabbi said that around two thousand years ago the Jews condemned the innocent Christ to death. And when they did that, they cried out: 'Let his blood fall on our heads and on our sons' heads.' Perhaps the time has come for that... ." (Claude Lanzmann, *Shoah: An Oral History of the Holocaust*, p. 100, New York, Pantheon, 1985) Thus, this Polish man finished his version of what had taken place during the war when the village's Jews were driven to their death.

When I first saw this episode in Lanzmann's *Shoah*, I couldn't believe my eyes and ears. The story as told by this Pole could never have taken place. Who can imagine a rabbi speaking such nonsense? Nevertheless, the Pole in the film, some forty plus years after the war, was actually convinced that the rabbi had said something that obviously reflected, not what the rabbi had said, but his own view as to why the Jews were punished by God. This is the deeply rooted cause of the Poles' hatred of the Jews—the fanaticism preached by the Polish Roman Catholic Church.

But it is always a mistake to generalize. Not every Pole thinks and feels this way. For instance, our partner in the joint venture I just mentioned, Karol Pavlek and his wife Anichka, are different. This nice religious Catholic couple with three lovely children, all very well brought up, have a liberal political and cultural outlook. Karol twice visited the site of Auschwitz-Birkenau, once even with a German associate of his. Together, Karol and I went to pay our homage to the Jews slaughtered by the Germans, visiting the site of the extermination camp in Treblinka near Warsaw.

♦

When we finally arrived in Krosno, we heard rumors that there were trucks of the free Czech Armed Forces, which were leaving to cross the Carpathian mountain chain in the general direction of Hungary. As it turned out, this information was correct. We somehow found the military base where they were stationed. The Czech soldiers were very cooperative and allowed our small group to travel with them. We boarded the trucks and started our journey into the mountains.

The trucks were traveling relatively fast and by nighttime we had already passed the border and were high up in the mountains and into Slovakia. Among the people who were in our truck were a young Jewish man and woman. They must have been in their early twenties. They were both, just like me, recently liberated from a concentration camp. They must have met only a week or so before but they had fallen in love. One has to understand that our deep emotions had survived only by some miracle. No wonder this couple fell in love or at least thought they were in love. I heard them talk about marrying and traveling right away to Romania on their way to *Eretz Yisrael*. They were two nice young people.

In our small group there was now also a doctor, a Hungarian Jewish medical doctor, also liberated from a concentration camp, on his way to his hometown in western Hungary on the Austrian border. He was a terrible person. Selfish, bad mouthed, cursing and grumbling constantly. One couldn't even imagine that a doctor was aware of such foul language.

Anyhow, we stopped for the night and found shelter in a small dwelling. Only an old Slovak woman lived there. It was a very primitive house. It didn't even have a chimney and the smoke was only ventilated when the door was open. (Only in 1998 in Kenya, in one of the small villages, did I again see similar primitive housing.) The smoke was hurting our eyes but there was no alternative and we went to sleep. I was awakened by the loud cursing of our doctor. The young couple apparently tried to make love during the night and the doctor was complaining and cursing that "because of their fucking I can't sleep". It was very rude of the doctor considering that they were a nice couple, whom all of us liked.

But let's jump twenty-two years ahead to April 1967. I was about to travel with my boss, Shalom Yoran, to the U.S. on behalf of Israel Aircraft Industries. In those days, I frequently worried about my heart. One day before leaving for New York, I was walking in Tel Aviv on Chen Boulevard and decided that I wanted to see a doctor. I saw a sign for a heart specialist and on the spur of the moment, I made up my mind to go and see him.

Nobody else was waiting to enter the doctor's office, so I walked right through and met him. Something was familiar about him. I seemed to know him from somewhere. I am blessed or maybe cursed by a good memory for faces. Judith, my companion for life, can testify that I recognize people in the mall, in the theater or on the street who I haven't seen for forty or even fifty years. Now that I am older and have fewer scruples than in my younger days, I usually walk up to these people and remind them of the place and time that we met. Anyhow, then in 1967, I slowly came to realize that this doctor must be the same one whom I remembered with such loathing from our trip across the Carpathian Mountains. I saw that he noticed the tattooed number on my arm and there was a strange look (of recognition?) in his eyes.

I didn't feel comfortable about leaving right away, which might be explained by my still relatively young age at the time. I think today in a similar situation I would either confront the person with the facts, as I remembered them or just walk away. However, then in 1967, I stayed and addressed him, as I would have any other doctor. I told him about my upcoming journey to the U.S. and the suspicion that I had about my heart. He examined me and confirmed my anxiety. "Yes," he said. "You are right. You have a serious health condition and were you younger (I was 37 years old then) I would recommend immediate surgery." He continued, "I don't advise you to travel. I am about to receive some new equipment that should allow me to make an even more thorough analysis of your heart. You should return right away when I receive this equipment." I told him that I would travel anyhow. I have to admit that, having recognized him as the person from the Carpathian Mountains way back in February 1945, I didn't believe a word he said about my health and had no intention of going to see him again. In parting, he provided me with the EKG he had just made as a "passport of my heart" should I need a medical record in case of emergency while in the U.S. Then, with a thick pen, he "corrected" the EKG and gave it to me. I don't know what his alterations intended to achieve but I am sure that there was some sinister intention behind it. Whoever heard of a doctor going through an EKG with a thick pen? He was obviously still an evil person, just as I remembered him.

I have never seen him and hopefully won't see him again. Since I am already close to eighty and he must have been some twenty years older than I at the time, the chances of us meeting in this life are slim.

BACK "HOME" IN HUNGARY

After that night in the hut with no chimney in the Carpathian Mountains, I was somehow able to board a small locomotive moving very slowly through the mountains. With other passengers, I rode on top of the locomotive itself. It was a very old machine. We were sitting on some sort of a balustrade just behind the chimney, which released a thick, black smoke right in our faces.

After some additional travel days, I crossed the Hungarian border at a town called Sátoraljaújhely, not that there was any sign of this being the border. The whole area was under Soviet occupation, so it didn't matter whether one was in Poland, the Czechoslovak Republic or Hungary. After an additional day on another train, I was close to Nyiregyháza, the town where I was born. At that last stage of my journey, I was totally exhausted; I didn't know how many days I hadn't slept. I had no strength left at all. I was lying on the floor inside the train, this time, a regular passenger car, letting everyone step over me. I didn't care, as long as I could catch a little sleep.

It was late evening or night when the train arrived in Nyiregyháza. The train station was in ruins. It had been severely bombed by the Allies during the war. It was dark, so I couldn't see the shape our house was in. As I have related, our home was located a few meters from the railroad station. Later, I observed that the whole general area of the station was in ruins except for our house—by some miracle, it wasn't hit by the bombs.

Arriving that night, I don't remember how I got information about where to go. I was directed to a house in town where Jews, who had already returned from deportation, were sleeping. Even at that early stage after liberation, while the war was still raging elsewhere, there were already the beginnings of local Jewish organizing.

In the year 2000, we had a gathering in one kibbutz in Israel for all the ex-residents of Nyiregyháza. From what some of those present at that meeting related, I got the impression that the house where I spent my first night upon returning to Nyiregyháza was the town bordello of former and better times. There was no vacant bed in the house so I slept on the floor, which didn't bother me too much.

Next morning, I was told that the Hahn family wanted me to come to stay with them. They had already heard, apparently from Pista Lipkovits, that I was alive and on my way home. I started out immediately for 121 Szarvas Street where the Hahn family lived. The route was very familiar. After all, we had lived in that house from the day I was born until I was ten years old.

When they had married, my parents rented the house from Mr. Dezső Hahn, the head of the family. The Hahns had obtained the house as a dowry from his wife's parents, the Lederers. It consisted of three small living rooms, a kitchen, a tiny maid's room and a pantry. There was neither a bathroom nor running water. In the yard, there was an outhouse and a well that supplied water for the household. The Lederers had several children, among them two daughters, Rezsi and Manci. Manci was married to Dezső Hahn. Rezsi was deported to Auschwitz-Birkenau and never returned. The Hahn family's only son, Emil, was my friend. The Hahns had not been deported even though they were Jewish. Dezső Hahn had been an exceptionally and highly decorated officer in the Austro-Hungarian Army during the Great War (the First World War). Because of his distinguished war record, the whole Hahn family enjoyed special status even after the Germans occupied Hungary in 1944. They were exempted from wearing the yellow star and also from moving to the ghetto and from the deportation, which followed. When Ferenc Szálasi, the leader of the Hungarian Nazi Arrow Cross party came to power in October 1944, all these special status privileges were canceled, but luckily, the authorities in Nyiregyháza conveniently forgot about the Hahn family and didn't bother them.

Nyiregyháza changed hands twice. The Red Army occupied it in October and then the Germans retook it. In November 1944, Nyiregyháza was finally liberated by the Red Army and the Hahns were saved. So, on March 6, 1945, the morning after my first night back in Nyiregyháza, I came to the gate at 121 Szarvas Street. There was a dog barking in the yard and after a while I heard the noise of a key being inserted in the lock and turned. In front of me stood Dezső Hahn who asked me who I was looking for, in the way one would address a complete stranger. Mr. Hahn obviously didn't recognize me because of my run-down condition and the rags I was wearing.

I didn't say a word; I was so surprised that he didn't recognize me despite the fact that he was expecting me. I saw in his eyes that he was slowly starting to recognize this "beggar" standing before him. He was so enraptured that he could hardly speak. One had to know Dezső Hahn to understand what an unsentimental person he usually was. His nature and regular behavior was just the opposite of anything sentimental. Recovering from his surprise, and speaking hoarsely, maybe even with tears in his eyes, he invited me in. Thus, my stay with the Hahns began.

On the day of my arrival, they prepared a feast for me consisting of meat, potatoes and thick gravy. Naturally, I got terrible diarrhea just like after the Christmas meal in Jaworznow. Later, I found out that quite a number of ex-*Häftlings* died after liberation from having eaten food that was too heavy.

The Hahn couple slept in the main bedroom, as had my parents back in the 1930s. Emil and I slept in the small bedroom, which, in "our time", used to be my grandfather's bedroom and became my bedroom after he passed away. The third room, which in our case had been the salon, i.e., the most elegant room with a piano, was now a sort of workshop housing cages for angora hares that served as the Hahns' sole income.

Emil did most of the work caring for the hares—feeding, cleaning, removing the hair with steel combs and selling it to be turned into wool. His mother, Manci, assisted him. Dezső was unfortunately very ill, having contracted tuberculosis earlier in his life. He was severely sick and often spat blood. There were days when he spent the whole time in bed, not being strong enough to get up.

In 1980 at UCLA in Los Angeles, I was taking some medical tests necessary for acceptance to the university's MBA program, when, to my surprise, I was informed that I must have had tuberculosis in the past because there were some scars on my lungs. It is possible that I contracted the disease without realizing it while living with the Hahns.

Because Dezső was practically immobilized, Emil and his mother were responsible for generating the family income. Emil was, and still is, a very gifted and talented person. He is very intelligent and good with his hands. Nowadays, as I write this story, he is Dr. Emil Hahn, retired Dean of the Electronics Faculty at the Budapest University of Technology and Economics, an internationally respected institute of technology.

Emil and I were good friends despite the age difference, which, of course, now that we are both in our seventies, has no meaning at all. Emil was born in 1927 and I am three years younger. We have known each other from the time I was born. My nickname was Karcsi, but, as a toddler, I couldn't pronounce it properly, so Emil would tease me with the name, "Tacsi". He would call me from a distance of some ten meters, sort of singing to me, "Tacsi, Tacsi, Tacsi", and I would reply in the same tone "Miche, Miche, Miche." Emil reminded me of this at his home in Buda in 1987 when we met again after forty-two years of no contact at all between us.

We were friends but also a little like rivals, which is not uncommon among boys (maybe even among adults). Although Emil was three years older, he was only two grades above me in Polgari High School where we jointly wrote, edited, printed and sold (although not too many) the school's student newspaper, *Csengetes utan* (After the Bell). Emil lost a year because he had moved to Yugoslavia during the 1930s. Then, he lost an additional year when he transferred to the gymnasium and had to study supplementary subjects (like Latin, for instance), which had been taught at his previous school but not at Polgari. One should not forget that he was working with the angora hares all those years as well. Therefore, despite the three-year age difference between us, he was only one grade above me at the gymnasium in 1945.

Emil was somewhat attracted to the unusual and also liked to help the weaker person. Before the deportations to Auschwitz, Emil was among the few boys, very few, if any, who befriended Jancsi Fried, whose tragic misadventure in Birkenau I have already described. They were in the same class at Polgari. I remember that Emil and I visited Jancsi in his home several times. It was typical of Emil to cultivate such a friendship and he sought to help Jancsi in many respects. When school opened again in April 1945, we returned to the gymnasium and it wasn't long before Emil found a girlfriend, a bright, non-Jewish young woman who was a bit lame.

During the months that I was living with the Hahns, our relationship had its ups and downs, primarily because of the attitude of Emil's father. Because Dezső was immobilized most of the time and was a charismatic person he behaved as a tyrant towards his family. Dezső, for instance, kept a tight control of his wife's daily activities. He interrupted her whenever this quiet, good-hearted, nice-looking woman, Manci, was trying to converse a little with one of the town's women passing by the window, which opened to the street.

Dezső behaved even worse towards his only son, Emil. If possible, he would have Emil around the house all the time. Once, Emil and I were building a model airplane and wanted to go to the field to fly and test it. Dezső opposed our trip. "Shoe sole is expensive," he used to say. "You are not supposed to walk too much lest it become worn and will have to be replaced... ." However, in all honesty, I have to admit that Dezső's attitude towards me was the most tolerant of the whole household. It would have been quite unnatural had this preference of Dezső not affected the relationship between Emil and me. I am not sure that Emil was too happy to have me at their house.

I think that Dezső's attitude toward me was thoroughly selfless, with no materialistic interest involved. I say this even though he was repeatedly inquiring about the possible hiding place of my family's "treasure". I kept telling him that as far as I knew, and I thought that I had been in the picture about my family's wealth or rather lack of it, we had no hidden treasure. By "treasure" Dezső meant hard currency and jewelry.

Thinking about such "treasure" lately, I have to admit that I have started to have my doubts. Maybe there was something hidden somewhere. There are two reasons behind my revised attitude. First, from re-reading the letters my parents wrote to Öcsi and Edit (my uncle and aunt) during the 1940s, which Edit and I rediscovered in an old shoebox in Edit's pantry. Some of these letters described the lawsuit my mother and Öcsi were jointly conducting against the older Kallai, brother to the prime minister, and the money my parents received at the successful conclusion of that lawsuit. This Kallai had a family ranch near Nyiregyháza and was an ardent card player. As I already recounted, my grandfather, my mother's father, was chief waiter or so-called pay waiter at the Korona in Nyiregyháza. In those days, only the chief waiter handled the money in a large establishment like the Korona. Therefore, he always had to have ready cash on hand. Whenever Kallai was losing at cards he borrowed money from my grandfather, from his own private funds. Kallai gave my grandfather IOUs but rarely paid him back. So when my grandfather passed away, quite a large amount of Kallai's debt was still outstanding. My mother and Öcsi knew about it and decided to sue Kallai.

This was no easy decision. For Jews to sue a gentry person of Kallai's caliber was no small matter. It is difficult to believe and it does justice to the Hungarian court that it decided in my family's favor. I remember the trial, although I must have been only about eleven years old (and the quarrels with the lawyer, a Mr. Boem I think, about his fee). So eventually, my family received some cash and, according to the letters to Öcsi and Edit, my parents were contemplating buying a house. However, they never did so and, in consequence, must have been left with money or some other valuables. Thus, it is possible that there was some sort of "treasure" hidden somewhere.

Another particular incident also makes me think that there might have been some valuables hidden away. There was a young man whose parents used to own a grocery store on the corner of Szarvas and Vecsei Streets. He returned from deportation during the late spring or early summer of 1945. When I met him, I noticed with some astonishment that he seemed to be disappointed in seeing me alive. I also vaguely recall him hinting that he had some information about my father's fate in the concentration camp. However, he didn't reveal anything to me. It is possible that he found out something about the hiding place of our valuables and was disappointed that, because of my survival, it would be more difficult for him to lay his hands on such treasure. He may have thought, wrongly, that I knew where it was.

But these are only assumptions and hypotheses about any valuables which my family might or might not have had hidden somewhere. The fact is that I didn't locate any treasure, although later, in the early summer of 1945, I did collect some furniture, clothing, etc. that belonged to my family. But I will report about this later in my story. As far as Dezső Hahn was concerned, I am quite certain that when he was talking about locating valuables which belonged to my parents he wasn't thinking to benefit from them himself, but merely to pursue this matter with my welfare in mind. As far as I know, the Hahns never received a penny for my upkeep in the months I spent in their home and that the sole reason for caring for me was their *Menshlichkeit* (human kindness), for which I am forever grateful.

Despite the fact that the Hahns treated me as one of the family, or even better, as I have already described, my morale was very low. The main reason was, of course, that my parents hadn't returned. As a matter of fact, I wasn't even able to obtain any reliable information about their fate from the people who did return from deportation. Nobody seemed to have any information about them. Maybe there was someone, among those who returned, who knew about either my mother or my father, but didn't want to be the bearer of bad news.

The only exceptions were three women from the Horowitz/Kara family—Rozsi Wirtschafter-Horowitz, Ili Horowitz and Edit Kara. Rozsi and Ili were sisters and Edit, about sixteen years old, was their niece. Rozsi was one of the two better friends of my mother. The other was Magda Tarján-Szölősi, about whom I will relate later. Rozsi married Elemér Wirtschafter, my father's childhood friend. The match between Rozsi and Elemér was initiated by my parents who were quite active in bringing together couples in need of friendly assistance.

There was a time when my mother, Rozsi and Ili tried to learn English together, planning to immigrate to some English-speaking country after the war. I remember Ili jokingly pronouncing our name, Sichermann, as "Sy-chuir-man".

Rozsi and Elemér had a little boy by the name of Gábor. This child must have been a little less than six years old at the time the Germans occupied Hungary in 1944. Neither Elemér nor Gábor survived Auschwitz. The parents of the Horowitz sisters and those of Edit Kara also perished, as did Ili's husband. (I reported about their marriage in the ghetto at the beginning of my story.) Therefore, one can imagine the morale and mood of these women when I met them in the early summer of 1945. These three were together in the concentration camp and I suppose this assisted them in surviving the hell they suffered. They told me that they saw my mother alive upon arrival in Birkenau and even later in the summer of 1944 when she was in reasonably good shape. They said that the second time they saw her she had even put on some weight, which for me was improbable, to say the least.

This was all the information I received from them about my mother. Again, I don't know whether they knew her fate but kept quiet because they were sorry for me or whether they really didn't know anything more.

Rozsi and Edit immigrated to Australia. I next met Rozsi in Israel in 1965 when she was visiting one of her relatives there. She was lying ill on a sofa when I went to see her. She had remarried and had a new family but I don't think she had ever overcome the tragedy of losing her son Gábor and her husband Elemér. She had had a very happy and harmonious marriage despite the fact that it was a late and arranged one.

I also met Ili a number of times in Paris. She also remarried a man from Nyiregyháza. They emigrated to join his brother in France who was in the clothing business. Jenő knew them from his work as a tailor. When I visited, the brothers already owned quite a large workshop manufacturing various ladies' garments. Ili and her husband had two or three grown-up sons by that time in the 1970s and were enjoying a happy and prosperous life.

I liked both Rozsi and Ili, especially Ili who was a happy person by nature. In pre-1944, as a young woman in Nyiregyháza, she was always in a good mood. I like smiling people. Ili still seemed to be an optimist when I met her in France as a mother with grown-up sons.

The case of the Horowitz sisters and their cousin Edit Kara is not the only case I know of women who stayed together in the concentration camp, helped each other, and thereby increased their chances of survival. Judith, who shares her life with me now, also survived Birkenau together with her mother Ibolya and her aunts Mancika and Etu. In my opinion, fate and Ibolya's motherly instincts saved the life of her son, Tomi/Zwi, and most probably her own and Judith's life as well.

The Roth family, Dezső, Ibolya, Vera/Judith and Tomi/Zwi were living in Munkács (Mukačevo, Czechoslovakia prewar; today Mukachevo in Ukraine) in 1944 when the Germans occupied Hungary. Munkács had been returned to Hungary from the dying Czecho-Slovak Republic in 1938.

While in the Munkács Ghetto, the Roths decided that they would try to escape to Budapest where they rightly believed it would be easier to survive than in Munkács. The family did indeed succeed in escaping from the ghetto by hiding in the alcove of the former house of one of the grandparents. They planned to rent a taxi or two in order to be driven to Budapest. One late afternoon, a taxi arrived already occupied by another Jewish family. There was just one place left in the taxi for the Roth family. The mother decided that her son Tomi would travel and pushed him into the car. Tomi was only nine years old at the time! The Roths were hoping that the next day a second taxi would come to take the rest of the family to Budapest. Unfortunately, the second car never arrived.

The taxi with Tomi left Munkács and a couple of days later arrived safely in Budapest. The other family who shared the taxi with Tomi delivered him to one of the Roth family relatives in Budapest. Tomi, in the weeks and months that followed didn't have it easy, far from it, but he eventually survived the war and was liberated by the Soviets in Budapest.

Why is this story so remarkable? Well, I will try to explain.

When Ibolya pushed Tomi into the taxi, the fate of many who were still alive at that time (and also those to be born later) was affected. Had Tomi not been sent to Budapest, he would not have survived Birkenau as a child of nine. There is also a high probability that Tomi would have been sent directly to the gas chambers upon arrival in Birkenau. Vera's chances of survival as a girl of only thirteen in Auschwitz would also have been diminished without the protection of her mother.

However, both Vera and Tomi survived. They immigrated to Israel and, between the two of them, have seven children, among them an agronomist, a computer expert, a heart specialist, an electrical engineer and a psychologist, and so far eight wonderful grandchildren. Without Ibolya's instinct in sending Tomi in the taxi, all these generations of bright men and women would have been lost. Just imagine the magnitude of the future Jewish generations lost because of the six million murdered in the Holocaust!

◆

During the spring of 1945, my morale in Nyiregyháza was very low. I felt that there was no hope of my parents returning. Unfortunately, my instincts in this regard were correct. My mother and father perished in the hell of the Nazi extermination campaign against the Jewish people.

There was a time then when I even considered suicide. I remember myself standing in front of the house at 121 Szarvas Street and contemplating climbing to the top of the tallest building in Niyiregyháza and jumping. The tallest building was Luther House where I used to have my piano lessons with Mrs. Führer, but it only had three floors. I don't think my suicidal thoughts were too serious; I didn't even take a single step in the direction of the Luther building. Maybe I was just feeling sorry for myself.

School started at the beginning of April 1945, about a month after I returned. I was now a student in the fifth grade of the Kossuth Gymnasium.

I rejoined school with the same classmates I had studied with before all hell broke loose with the German occupation of Hungary on March 19, 1944. The same boys, but without my friend Pista Klein, who never returned from deportation, and without Andris Citrom whom I have also mentioned before. Andris had enrolled in the gymnasium right after we graduated from elementary school at a time when all the other Jewish boys went to the less prestigious Polgari High School. Andris perished in Mauthausen.

Anyhow, in the spring of 1945, I started to study again with the non-Jewish boys and girls (in 1945, boys and girls started to attend the same class) who had spent the last twelve months in Nyiregyháza while I was away, you know where. Not that there was much sympathy toward me, considering what I had gone through, from the boys who knew me from the previous year. On the contrary, one of them, a fairly stupid and slightly physically disabled student by the name of Csele, kept assuring me that the Germans were reoccupying part of Hungary and that we would soon see them again in Nyiregyháza. Since he was disabled, I couldn't even allow myself to hit him.

Among the girls who now studied in the class, there were two young Jewish women from Budapest. Because food supply to the capital at that time was still very meager, these two (unrelated) girls from wealthy families were sent to stay temporarily in Nyiregyháza where food was more readily available.

I fell in love with one of them, called Yvette. She was a silent, maybe also a little arrogant, plump maid. I have to confess that my feelings were not at all reciprocated. The other girl, called Zsuzsi, did show signs, maybe, of wanting to get friendly with me, but as is usually the case in such situations, one always runs after the "unobtainable" and is indifferent to the more readily "obtainable". Anyhow, as I later found out in Budapest, there was much snobbishness to be found in well-to-do Jewish youth circles.

Among the boys from out of town, there was a non-Jewish boy from the Buda district of Budapest, also apparently from a well-to-do family. We befriended each other a little, which in itself was exceptional because Jewish boys didn't have gentile friends. After school, he sometimes accompanied me home to the Hahn's. I remember a sort of admiration in his voice as he described the way half drunken Russian soldiers in Buda conducted their house-to-house fighting against the Germans.

It was a very short school year, only three months. But I learned a lot. I started writing, reading and speaking some French. This knowledge later helped me during the sixties and seventies when I spent time in France with the French Air Force and the French Aeronautical Industry. I also learned biology for the first time. This knowledge, assisted by some *chutzpah*, allowed me to give lectures on the subject to my group of children in Strüth, Germany, in 1946–1947. After school, I also attended Hebrew lessons given by a Zionist teacher who had returned from a Hungarian forced-labor camp.

I went with Emil Hahn to the same school although he was one grade above me. But Hebrew lessons, I attended alone. The Hahn family was not inclined to Zionism. It might be too far-fetched to claim that Dezső, although a Jew himself, was a little antisemitic, but I don't think that he was too far from it. In any case, Hungarian culture was very close to the heart of the Hahn family, as had been the case with most of the Jewish Hungarian middle class before the war. This trend changed considerably after the liberation in 1945, but some Jewish families like the Hahns felt closer to Hungarian socialism than to anything connected to their Jewish origins. Therefore, it is no wonder that I eventually found myself in Israel while Emil made his career in Hungary.

Dezső Hahn passed away in the early summer of 1945. As a matter of fact, just before his death he was feeling so well that he walked all alone a couple of times from his home to the municipality, a distance of around three kilometers. He was interested in local politics. During one of those occasions, whether during his walk or while in the Mayor's office, Dezső suffered a heart attack and collapsed. He was immediately hospitalized and after two or three days passed away.

During the spring of 1945 my family's good friends Magda and Ernő Tarján (Teitelbaum) also returned to Nyiregyháza. Magda lived in Budapest and luckily survived there the events of 1944. Her parents perished in Auschwitz as did her brother Laci and her two sisters. One of the sisters had a lovely little girl of seven or eight years old who also was murdered in Auschwitz. The other sister was a spinster. Magda's other two brothers, Gyuri and Pista, survived. Both eventually settled in Israel. I met Pista in December 1948 in Haifa when he had just arrived from Cyprus. Ernő and Magda, together with their adopted son Eytan, came to live in Israel as well after the 1956 Hungarian uprising. Ernő had been a member of the Zionist movement in his youth. Still, I think that Ernő and Magda decided to immigrate to Israel mainly because antisemitism had raised its ugly head again right after the Hungarians felt free to demonstrate their true feelings toward the Jews still living in Hungary. The slogan of some of the wall graffiti was *"Izig most nem viszünk Auschwitzig"*, which roughly translates to "Itzig, this time it won't even be necessary to take you to Auschwitz." It meant that, "this time we will butcher you Jews here in Hungary." The Tarjáns told me that just before leaving Nyiregyháza, in the fall of 1956, they slept in their house with an ax by the pillow for eventual self-defense.

Magda was my mother's best friend when both of them were young and unmarried. They attended a sewing class together. Magda knew me as a newborn baby. When I started to talk, I couldn't properly pronounce her name and called her Manya néni (Aunt Manya). Magda was very proud that she had known me so early in my life and used to repeat it again and again, especially after my daughters, Michal and Merav, were born.

Ernő had a good sense of humor. He was my father's friend and an even closer friend of my Uncle Öcsi. As bachelors, Öcsi and Ernő lived in a small apartment in Budapest together with Feri Heller. Feri was another special type of person. He also had a good, though somewhat black, sense of humor. Ernő knew and admired Edit, who later became Öcsi's wife. Ernő liked to eat well and after the engagement of Öcsi and Edit was regularly invited for lunch or dinner to Edit's family. Juliska Lakos, Edit's mother, was a first-class cook. Ernő used to say to Juliska, "It is a pity that you haven't got a second daughter like Edit, I would gladly marry her."

The Lakos family had only one daughter, Edit, and therefore Ernő had to try his luck elsewhere. Here is where my parents entered the picture. They arranged for Magda and Ernő to meet. And as they say, "the rest is history". The marriage took place in 1943. My parents and I attended together with many guests in the Szöllősi home of Magda's parents.

Soon after the marriage, the young couple had to part. Ernő was drafted and Magda moved to Budapest. They were reunited in Nyiregyháza right after the war, having luckily survived its atrocities. One of Ernő's eyes was artificial, made of glass. As a youth he had lost it in a fight with, you guessed it, an antisemite.

After arriving in Israel, the Tarjáns settled in Holon. They first rented, then bought, a nice little apartment there and Ernő got a good job as a bookkeeper in a large Israeli company. It was then that he started to have problems with his one good eye. Bookkeeping strains the eyes and Ernő panicked about endangering his only eye and maybe losing it as well. Because of this worry, he eventually quit his job and unfortunately regressed into a deep melancholy from which he never completely recovered. Responsibility for the Tarján family's well being was thus entrusted to Magda's care. To my great surprise and delight, she rose to the challenge and became the acting head of the family. Magda succeeded in caring for their son Eytan as well as safeguarding Ernő's prestige as the formal head of their little family, despite his condition.

Before I go on, I have to say a few more words about Feri Heller, my Uncle Öcsi's roommate. Feri used to be my father's colleague in Nyiregyháza and was let go by the firm following the anti-Jewish legislation, which limited the number of Jews one could employ. He moved to Budapest and made his living by writing books, or rather pamphlets, about the Wild West and cowboys. As a young man he had a good sense of humor but was also a very pessimistic person. I have heard that some of the best humorists are pessimists.

One particular incident involving Feri has stuck in my mind all these years. I recall that in 1942 or 1943, while serving in one of the Hungarian Army's forced labor units on the Eastern Front, he somehow got a leave of absence for a few days and came to visit my parents in Nyiregyháza. We were sitting around the stove, it was winter at the time, and Feri was telling us that the Germans were forcing the Jews in the Ukraine to dig their own graves and then executing and burying them there.

After Feri left our home that evening there was a long silence. Nobody, neither my father nor my mother spoke. Eventually, they recovered from the shock of what they had just heard and uttered, "Oh, Feri is a nice person, but he is known to always be very pessimistic, seeing the dark side of everything."

I think that this was a typical reaction to hearing the truth about something that one finds too horrible to believe. The Jews of Hungary, as human beings who usually behave to psychologically protect themselves, were afraid to face reality. After all, even during the war, there were sources of information for those who wanted to know about the true fate of the Jews. For instance, there were in Hungary a number of Polish-Jewish refugees in hiding. They must have known and relayed to some Hungarian Jews the facts about the ghettos and the concentration camps and what was going on there. It is conceivable that information about Auschwitz and the mass murder of Jews in the Soviet Union trickled through the iron-clad curtain of Nazi secrecy and dissimulation. However, the Hungarian Jews deluded themselves into believing that, "this could never happen here, and will never happen here."

I saw Feri briefly on the streets of Budapest in the summer of 1945 and then met him in Israel in the 1970s. He was visiting some relatives of his wife and we took him out for dinner. His sense of humor, unfortunately, had gone. I don't think he enjoyed much his visit to Israel and staying with his wife's family. I tried to remind him of the above story, which has remained so significant to me despite all the years that have passed. To my great disappointment, he didn't remember anything about it. Well, of course, in the 70s, Feri Heller was already quite old.

♦

During the summer of 1945 in Nyiregyháza, the Tarjáns tried to convince me to leave the Hahn family and move to their home even while Dezső Hahn was still alive. The truth is that there was no sympathy lost between these two families. My infrequent visits to the Tarjáns were not very welcomed in the Hahn household. However, after Dezső passed away, it was quite obvious that I should be moving on and there was no objection raised to my leaving for the Tarjans. I collected my very few belongings and walked to the former Szöllősi residence. Magda and Ernő lived in quite a big house at 5 Katóna Street, a street that was muddy and neglected. Even in 1987, when I first returned to Nyiregyháza, the street was still in the same shape with no pavement, just as I remembered it from 1945.

A little while later, Pista Szöllősi returned from one of the Hungarian Army's forced labor units and came to live with his sister. Pista was neither too intelligent nor very diligent. In school, it was well known that his grades were always very low and he barely managed to even pass from grade to grade. I doubt that he finished much more than the four grades of Polgari. Magda used to tell me that Pista made her angry because he was so different from their father who was a clever, cultured man with a distinguished career in the Hungarian Ministry of Finance. Still, I appreciated Pista because he entertained me with piquant stories and jokes.

By the summer, almost all the survivors of deportation had returned to Nyiregyháza. I met Mrs. Altmann and Mrs. Weishaus, mothers of my friends and former classmates, Gyuri Altmann and Tomi Weishaus whom I have mentioned above. These women, who were left all alone because neither their husbands nor their sons returned, suffered from a terrible lack of morale.

The mother of Laci Kuhn, another friend of mine, was more fortunate. Although the father didn't survive, Laci, who was an only child, returned after

Jaworznow, Blechhammer and Mauthausen, as did his mother. Eventually, both of them immigrated to Israel where Laci, the only Jewish boy in school who could draw a decent picture, became quite a well-known painter. As I recently found out, not only was Laci's first wife a Hungarian Jew herself and a painter but, according to them, their son, now living in London, is a much more gifted painter than the parents.

I also saw Adolf Klein in Nyiregyháza. He recognized me but we didn't speak. He was the father of my friend Pista Klein. Pista and his mother perished in Auschwitz and I suppose Adolf couldn't bring himself to talk to me. The pain of losing his younger son was still too vivid in the summer of 1945. Laci, Pista's older brother, returned and both Adolf and Laci later made *Aliya*. In the 1960s, I met Adolf in Ramat Gan, in Israel, during one of the Nyiregyháza reunions. Those reunions were held annually on the anniversary of our deportation to Auschwitz. This time we spoke. I reminded Adolf of my friendship with his son. He remembered it very well. I was an Air Force Lieutenant Colonel at the time and I saw in his eyes that when looking at me he was thinking of Pista.

Another person I remember meeting on the street at that time in 1945 was Emil Zsák. Mr. Zsák wasn't Jewish. He and my father had both worked for Futura. Zsák was higher up in the firm but my father was the "man in the field", i.e., he did the work. Emil Zsák respected my father and our two families even had some sort of a social relationship. However, such a relationship among Jews and gentiles was limited in scope. Every year after the Christmas holidays, we used to visit the Zsák home. They never disposed of the Christmas tree before we came to see it and they usually even had a Christmas present for me. They had two children, Zsuzsi, a year older than me, and Gyuri, a year younger. It was obvious that Mr. Zsák felt and looked very uncomfortable when we accidentally met on the street in 1945.

The Buji family behaved in a very similar fashion when I went to see them. Mr. Buji had "inherited" my father's job and the house we had lived in before the deportation. The house went with the job since it belonged to Futura.

One day, I went to see them in their (our) home. I no longer recall the reason for my visit. To get to the house one had to pass the courtyard gate facing the square, which was just across from the train station, and then along a small path and the veranda to enter the house either via the hall or the kitchen. Passing the gate, I was met by our dog, Abris, who somehow survived the bombings during the war. Abris started to jump up and down on me—he seemed to be angry and happy at the same time. He behaved as if he had gone crazy. He apparently wasn't sure about my identity. Am I somebody he knows or am I an intruder? Abris, barking, jumping and biting me in the process, accompanied me to the house. The whole Buji family was assembled in the living room, which only a little over a year before was still my room. The Bujis, just like Abris the dog, were uncomfortable and didn't know how to behave in my presence. It was their home now but as they were decent enough folks they must have realized that they had acquired the house and Mr. Buji's current job only because the Germans had murdered my father, an utterly innocent man.

My father and all the other Jews were executed, no, annihilated by the Germans. My father wasn't a soldier who was killed on the field of battle; he didn't perish by accident, he was exterminated by the Nazi beast and, one has to say, with the whole-hearted cooperation of the Hungarian authorities and most of the Hungarian people. That's how Mr. Buji got to inherit my father's job and our home, as well. No wonder that he and his family, wife, son and daughter, must have felt like intruders in my presence, in our home. Maybe I am deluding myself; maybe they didn't feel at all like intruders. Maybe they felt that it was we who were the intruders before March 1944, living in "their house" in "their country" and snatching from them "their jobs". Who knows what really went through their minds during my presence there. One thing I am sure of, they wanted me out of there as fast as possible, just as I also wanted to leave as soon as I could. I didn't stay there more than a few minutes and then left. I have never again set foot in the house nor did I ever see any of the Buji family again.

The only furniture belonging to us that remained in our old house was our piano. The Bujis said that Russian soldiers had defecated on the piano and that they had cleaned it up. I naively believed their story, but nowadays I wonder whether it were the Hungarians who, because of their hatred toward the Jews, did such a despicable act, or whether it was the Russians, with all the reason in the world to dislike the Hungarians whose army, in concert with the German *Wehrmacht* and SS, had devastated their country. Who knows; maybe the whole defecation and grand cleanup was just a story. Anyhow, I received a little bit of money from Futura as a last salary that was due to my father, which I gave to Dezső Hahn.

Some years later, in the 1950s, my mother-in-law, who at the time still lived in Hungary, went to visit the Tarján and the Hahn families in Nyiregyháza. I asked her to dispose of the piano, which was still in the possession of the Buji family, and she went to see them. Mrs. Buji asked vehemently that we leave the piano with them so as not to interfere with her daughter's piano lessons. I didn't agree and told my mother-in-law to sell the piano. So she took delivery of the piano and sold it. Later, I regretted that I didn't agree to let the Buji girl have the piano. They were not such a bad bunch. The terrible fate my family suffered wasn't their fault. Had I left the piano with them, at least I would have known where it was, and maybe could have even seen it on one of my visits after 1987 when I returned there for a visit.

While living with the Tarjáns, I started to collect some of my family's belongings dispersed all around town. I took a cart with a horse and went from place to place loading furniture, clothing, etc. Nowadays, I wonder how I was able to locate the people who had our belongings. Although, I recall that after the German occupation in the spring of 1944 and before they transferred us to the ghetto, I participated, riding a horse-driven cart, in dispersing some of our possessions with various acquaintances of my parents.

One incident testifies to my childish attitude while reclaiming our belongings. There was a family who had some of our belongings in their house. The man was the factory's stoker at Futura, and my father had been his boss. In the summer of 1945, with the Red Army's presence in Nyiregyháza, he declared himself a long-time Socialist. I don't know whether he was or wasn't, but he refused to return our things, hinting that my father was a bourgeois who exploited the working class. He was stealing our belongings in the name of Socialism.

I was angry and threatened that if he didn't return our belongings right away, I would go to the police. After all, he shouldn't get away with stealing our things because my father was a hero in 1919 during the Red regime of Béla Kun. I claimed proudly that in those days my father was, of all things, a counter-revolutionary. As a matter of fact, in the general lawlessness reigning in Hungary after World War I, when the Communist regime collapsed and the Horthy regime took over, my father participated in an ad hoc organization with the purpose of restoring some order. Because of this past activity, my father tried to obtain a special counter-revolutionary exemption status from the anti-Jewish measures imposed in 1944, but was unsuccessful.

However, for me to voluntarily attribute a counter-revolutionary status to my father, from as far back as 1919, while the armies of the Soviet Union were occupying Hungary in 1945, was both naive and very stupid. Luckily for me, someone quickly told me to hush up, keep quiet and not to brag about such an outdated matter. What I was trying to do could only be compared to the audacity of someone in Hungary, now in the 21st century, claiming to be an ardent admirer of the demised Soviet Union. As in the Latin epigram, "Sic transit gloria mundi", or roughly, "Thus passes glory from the world." Well, so much for that.

All our possessions that I was able to collect were stored in one of the vacant rooms in the home of Magda and Ernő. When I left for Budapest later that summer, I left everything with them. In 1957, the Tarjáns, arriving in Israel, brought with them what remained of the set of silverware, spoons, knives etc., which was part of my mother's trousseau upon her marriage to my father in 1929. Very negligently, in subsequent years, I lost some of this silver. We possess today only a few items of the original set. Everything else was left behind; maybe the Tarjáns sold everything or used it themselves, I don't know, I never inquired.

It was during those summer months that I made contact with my Aunt Edit in Budapest and she invited me to stay with her there. So one sunny morning in July, Ernő and I boarded the train and set out for Budapest. In those days, traveling by train was an adventure in itself, but we made it to the capital relatively smoothly and I ended up in Edit's home, which, at the time, was on Örömvölgy Street in Pest.

Before March 1944, Edit and Öcsi had lived in a tiny apartment on Andrássy Street, which was in a very elegant neighborhood and adjacent to the opera house. After the German occupation of Hungary, the Jews in Budapest were first made to move into special *Csillagos Haz* (houses with a Jewish star), and later, were either hoarded into the ghetto, deported into the Reich, or shot by the Hungarians, with their corpses thrown into the Danube. Edit and her baby girl, Vera, followed this same routine into the ghetto, but luckily escaped both deportation and the Danube.

After the liberation at the end of January 1945, Edit couldn't return to her home in Andrássy Street because the apartment was already occupied by a "bombed out" Hungarian gentile family. When Edit tried to claim her apartment, she was told by the authorities, or more precisely by one of the clerks deciding on her matter that "there is still enough space left in the Danube." Therefore, Edit and little Vera had no choice but to move in with Edit's parents, Vilmos and Juliska Lakos. The Lakos couple lived together with Frici (Juliska's sister) and her husband, Béla, in a three-story apartment building on Örömvölgy Street, which was jointly owned by the Juliska and Frici sisters.

My Uncle Öcsi had "disappeared" while serving in one of the forced labor units of the Hungarian Army. According to rumors, which later hit Edit's ears, Öcsi was murdered in the last days of the war somewhere in Austria.

Arriving in Budapest in July 1945, I moved in with Edit, Vera, Vilmos and Juliska, all in their one small apartment. Frici and Dezső occupied a similar-sized adjacent apartment. Edit and Vera slept in one of the bedrooms, Vilmos and Juliska in the second bedroom. My place was in the dining room where I slept on a collapsible bed.

No wonder the mood in the household was bad. I don't recall much smiling there; not that there was much reason for anyone to smile. Neither Öcsi nor Gyuri, Edit's brother, had returned after the war. The only person working and earning a meager salary at that time was Edit. She worked in the same store, owned by Mr. Baumgarten, where Öcsi had been employed as a bookkeeper. Later in the fall, Vilmos got a part-time job with the Jewish Joint organization. The Joint was helping the Jews by supplying some, but alas, not nearly enough, food. I myself, at least, was always hungry. I was to become fifteen years old in September and at that age a boy is always hungry. On some lucky Sundays, I managed to eat three lunches, one after the other. First at home, a very meager meal, then a second in a Jewish soup kitchen on Wesselényi Street and the third lunch in the home of the Steinberger family who were relatives of my Sichermann grandmother. Weekdays, I tried to eat two meals. I was so hungry that sometimes when Edit made noodles I snatched some of them raw while still on the wooden rolling board.

Just like during the war, or maybe even more so, there were "points" for everything—bread, flour, meat, milk, etc. Even so, there wasn't enough food reaching Budapest and if one wanted to ensure getting the rations allocated by points, it was still necessary to stand in line in front of the stores early in the morning before opening hours, before the supply ran out. Standing in line was my job. I had to get up early in the morning and wait in front of the grocery for my turn to buy bread and milk and bring it home.

Edit was very busy. During the day she worked at her job with Mr.

Baumgarten. She had to take care of Vera, who was a three-year-old, before leaving for her job and after coming home in the evening. In addition, Edit also had to look after me.

Inflation was raising its ugly head more and more and Edit's earnings couldn't suffice for even the barest of our needs. In those days after the war, most commerce was based on barter rather than purchase with paper money. I demonstrated my commercial talent (which since then has evaporated without a trace) when I exchanged a carpet for a radio. This carpet had been "mobilized" (a nice word for stolen) by Edit after the war in retaliation for her own carpet having been stolen by someone else.

I had the letter of introduction from Margit Höchtel to a female piano teacher at the Hungarian Academy of Music. I went to see her at her home in one of the more distinguished neighborhoods of Budapest. She made me play the piano for her and then agreed to teach me "for free" as her private student. This lady, who I think was Jewish, even arranged for a musical instruments store to lease me gratis a small piano, a so-called pianino. This piano was duly delivered to Örömvölgy Street, again, at no cost to us. Whether she did all this for me because she thought I had talent or because she felt sorry for me, I will never know. Although, I guess that the second supposition was stronger than the first one. Anyhow, I started to study with her and practice at home, but I have to admit that I wasn't, in any shape or form, able to enjoy it.

In August, Edit came with some big news. She had arranged a vacation for me by Lake Balaton. It turned out that, in order to participate, I had to become a member of the *Hanoar Hazioni* or *HanHaz*, one of the Zionist youth organizations functioning at the time in Budapest. I was enthusiastic about the idea, joined the *HanHaz* and quickly became friendly with some of the boys in the movement. In columns and rows of three, we would proudly march up and down through the streets of the city, although mostly in the more Jewish areas.

Then the great day came and we took the train to Lake Balaton. Our camp was set up in Balatonboglár, a little village on the shores of the lake. Just as we arrived and set up camp, the rains started. It rained for days. As there was not much leadership exercised by the seniors, there were no programs to keep us busy. We couldn't go swimming because of the weather, and so there was nothing much to do. Only some of the senior boys had some fun with the more popular girls.

The star among the girls was the very pretty Zsuzsi Grünspan. She was being raised by her grandmother and her own attractiveness was no secret to her. As a newcomer, I had no chance, so I didn't even make an attempt to introduce myself. Zsuzsi was obviously enjoying herself tremendously in Balatonboglár with all the boys flocking around her like bees around honey. Later in Israel, Zsuzsi married Robi Balla with whom I served in the Israeli Air Force from 1948 to 1950. Our two families became good friends and the friendship has endured the passing of the last 50 years. Robi and Zsuzsi recently celebrated their 50th wedding anniversary with all their family and friends.

Anyhow, while in Balatonboglár, I was very bored and decided to leave and return to Budapest. As I mentioned, it was very difficult to get a place on a train in those days. However, I somehow managed to board one, heading in my direction, but the only place available was on top of one of the cars just behind the locomotive. I was wearing a raincoat loaned to me by Edit. When I arrived in Budapest, I discovered to my horror that it was full of tiny holes caused by the sparks emitted through the chimney of the locomotive. The coat was completely destroyed and had to be thrown away. Nobody should envy me for the well-deserved dressing down I got from my aunt.

BACK IN SCHOOL

School started in September and I entered the 6th grade of the Jewish Abonyi Gymnasium. Its name comes from its location on Abonyi Street in Budapest. However, in the fall of 1945 its building wasn't restored yet from the war damage it had suffered. Therefore, we studied at an alternative location, namely on Wesselényi Street. There were two Jewish gymnasia in Budapest, one for boys and the other for girls. This segregation was maintained even after the war. However, the boys and girls studied in the same building although separately—girls in the morning and boys in the afternoon. It was very romantic to leave letters in the afternoon to be picked up by one of the opposite sex the next morning and vice versa. Only much later did I find out that my future wife, Sárkány, who was two grades below me, was in the very classroom in the morning where I was in the afternoon. As a matter of fact, we weren't even acquainted at the time.

Sárkány was a model student. She always earned the best grades in all subjects. Because her father had perished very early in the war, in 1942, her family's financial situation was grave. She was accepted into this very prestigious school and received a scholarship based on her merits. Sárkány was the star of her class.

I didn't at all enjoy going to that school. In Nyiregyháza, I was usually among the best students in my class, but in Budapest I was far from such a status. In addition, most of my classmates were unfriendly to me and some of them were outright snobs. During intervals between classes, political debates were conducted in a very pompous manner. A student full of his own self-importance would announce something like, "In the name of (such and such party, or such and such youth movement) I declare that... ." It was all so unreal for me, nothing like what I had encountered before.

I had only one friend, Robi Vermes, who was my former classmate in Nyiregyháza from first grade of elementary school to first grade in Polgari, after which the Vermes family returned to Budapest. We both must have been six years old when we first met in Nyiregyháza.

There were two peculiarities about Robi. First, he was the only boy I ever met who was from Budapest. Everybody else I knew was from Nyiregyháza, which for me, a six-year-old, was the center of the world. Secondly, Robi had very thick sensual lips, the like of which I had never seen before. Therefore, an "obvious" equation was born in my mind: people from Budapest have thick lips, or rather Robi has thick lips because he is from Budapest. I am quite ashamed to admit that for many years after first grade I still believed in this theory.

Robi was responsible for introducing me to the "facts of life". Once, while we were walking in the forest or participating in a Zionist meeting there, I am not sure which, he explained to me that kids are born because "some kind of fluid originating from that certain part of the man's body is introduced into the women's body". This is a true and precise quotation from what he said to me that day in the woods. I have to admit very frankly that I didn't understand, but was ashamed to ask, which "certain part of the body" Robi was referring to.

There was an additional and very important item about my friendship with Robi. The Vermes family lived in a lovely house on Kossuth Street. Whenever I visited Robi there, I had to behave exceptionally well because

Robi's mother was very strict about good manners. More importantly, though, every time I went to play with Robi at his home, the maid served us cocoa with whipped cream and cakes at five o'clock. At my home, cocoa was on the menu only on birthdays.

One never knows in life when one is lucky. Robi's father was the director of a steam mill in Nyiregyháza, but in 1940 he was fired from this important job because of the anti-Jewish legislation. I suppose that at the time the Vermes family felt that this was a tragedy. In the reality and the madness of that era, it turned out to be the luckiest event in their lives. This was because the Vermes family, originally from Budapest, moved back there as a result and thus escaped the deportation to come in 1944, when all the Jews of Nyiregyháza were deported to Auschwitz. In Budapest, however, about half the Jews survived, including the whole Vermes family (except Robi's father): the parents, my friend Robi who was the youngest child, his older brother Geza and sister Klari.

Robi, now mostly called Dönci (he had two first names, Robi and Ödön), made *Aliya* in 1949 or the early 1950s, and after graduating from the Hebrew University of Jerusalem, traveled to the U.S. to study for his Master's degree. He later ended up in Montreal, Canada, where he became professor of mathematics at McGill University. Geza became an engineer working for Lycoming, an aircraft engine manufacturer in the U.S., and Klari lives in Australia. I met Robi in Israel before he immigrated to Canada and I also visited him and his wife several times in Montreal. Once I even met his brother Geza there.

♦

Back to the fall of 1945 in Budapest and there was a boy in my class to whom I taught Hebrew after school. My Hebrew knowledge was less than minimal so before each "lesson" I had to prepare myself for the exact text we were going to study. My preparedness, therefore, was limited to the particular chapter we were to look at, and not one word beyond it. The parents of the boy knew this, but because their son was a hunchback and had no friends in class (I have already described the atmosphere in our class), they overlooked my limited knowledge of Hebrew. The main reason, therefore, they engaged me was to serve as companion to their son, if only for a few hours a week. Sometimes, I even took him to the mountains near Buda for short trips to have us enjoy the fresh air. I was paid very little money, but I was entitled to have lunch with them when I was teaching their son and we got delicious sandwiches for our trips.

All and all, I was miserable during that fall of 1945—hungry most of the time, not many friends to talk to and not very good in school. In addition, the mood at home, with Edit and her family, was quite oppressive.

From time to time, Edit and I went to the cinema together and to a small number of theater performances. On one such occasion, I remember well, we went to see a boring Russian film. My experience from those days was that most Russian films were amateurish and dull. There were Russian soldiers in the audience and the rest of the audience didn't conceal its dislike, or even its ridicule. The soldiers became angry. It was fast becoming quite dangerous to be in that cinema as one could not be sure what the soldiers might do. It was not unimaginable or even unheard of for them to even start shooting. In addition, Russian soldiers were not known to be sober all the time, quite the contrary. The audience soon realized that demonstrating any further criticism of Russian art could be bad for one's health and the rest of the film was endured in silence.

To walk home at night or even in the evening darkness was quite dangerous. Lawlessness and the unfriendly behavior of the Russian troops made it quite risky to be found on the streets of Budapest after dark. I don't know how true it was but one constantly heard stories about people being been beaten up and their belongings, even clothing, being taken off their bodies and stolen.

CHAPTER 4

THE JOURNEY TO ISRAEL

MY RETURN TO ZIONISM—THROUGH THE FRONT DOOR

I was restless, longing for the company of my own age group, maybe especially for the company of girls. I was looking for some enjoyment in my life. That's why I ended up visiting one *ken* or club of *Hashomer Hatzair*, which was my original Zionist youth movement back in Nyiregyháza. I don't recall how or by whom I was reintroduced, but I found myself in front of the door opening into the *ken* on Rakoczy Street in Pest. I opened the door and found the place full of dancing and singing girls and boys. One of the girls, I think her name was Bischitz, noticed my entrance.

I was a little stiff, which must have been obvious to everyone who looked at me. It only took a few moments for Bischitz to organize a small group for a "welcome" party. To ease my awkwardness, the group grabbed me, lifted me up and, with loud shouts of "hopla, hopla", threw me into the air, caught me and threw me into the air again. After this ritual was repeated several times, my stiffness was gone. For the first time since arriving in Budapest, I felt among friends.

It was only natural, therefore, that I decided on the spot to join this crowd. The central and most important subject on the agenda was always *Aliya*, realization of the *Shomer* dream to live in *Eretz Yisrael*. I didn't need much time or too much pondering to decide that I was also going to make *Aliya* as soon as possible.

I was lucky, I was told, because a large group consisting of a bunch of young girls and boys approximately my age was just getting organized to leave soon for *Eretz Yisrael*. I started to rush from office to office to arrange for my acceptance into this group and again was told that I was lucky because one of the younger boys had declined to go and I could have his place. I grabbed the opportunity and enlisted. I was all charged up to go.

I told Edit about my plans. She didn't raise much objection; she understood my misery and knew the hopelessness of her situation as well. Öcsi had tragically perished in the war and Edit, later in 1946, married Feri Rona, a Jewish man who had returned from the camps and had himself lost his family—wife and two children.

For a while Edit, Vera and Feri lived in a small village called Zalabaksa where Feri still owned some land and other property from before the war. Because the Communist regime, which in the meantime had been forced upon Hungary by the occupying Soviet forces, confiscated all of Feri's property, they had had to leave Zalabaksa and move back to Budapest. Edit gave birth to a wonderful second daughter, Gyöngyi, now herself a mother to three boys. Gyöngyi lives with her children and husband, Peter Fischer, in Vienna, Austria.

LEAVING HUNGARY

Before leaving Hungary on my way to *Eretz Yisrael* with the other Zionists, I still had one important errand to do for Edit and family. It was a very cold winter and food was very scarce in the capital. In the countryside, food was more readily available. I volunteered to travel to Nyiregyháza to bring back some potatoes, but finding reliable transportation was a big problem. I found a way, however. In the "good old" pre-March 1944 days we had the Gottesdien family as neighbors. Relative to us they were quite rich; they had a large plot of several acres with planks of wood stored there in very large quantities. They brought wood from the forests, cut it into planks, stored and sold it wholesale.

The Gottesdien family had two grown sons. Miklos (Gal) who was a medical doctor and Bandi (Gal) who must have had Communist affiliations because after the war he became one of the closest co-workers of the Jewish Communist mayor of Budapest, Zoltán Vas, and was responsible for food supply to the capital. Later in 1948, when the communists officially took control of the government, Vas became the minister in charge of economy. Miklos made *Aliya* while Bandi was nominated as Hungary's economic attaché in France. Bandi never returned to Hungary from France following this appointment. He, like so many other former idealists, became disillusioned with the communist regime and decided that it wasn't for him. Later, he even came to visit Israel to "test the water here" but finally returned to France. His daughter and family, however, live in Israel.

Anyhow, before my trip in the winter of 1945 to Nyiregyháza, I located Bandi in his office. He was a very busy man and judging from the crush of people in his office and telephones constantly ringing he obviously held an important job in Zoltán Vas's municipality. Bandi arranged for me to travel to Nyiregyháza in one of the Soviet Army trucks, which were on loan to the Hungarian authorities and designated to bring back food to the people of Budapest. I arrived safely in Nyiregyháza, with the truck dropping me off just a few meters from the Tarjans' house. It was already evening and dark by the time I knocked on their door. They were happy to see me and I spent the night there. The next day, I managed to buy a full sack of potatoes, which I dragged to the railroad station looking for transportation back to Budapest. The only train leaving for the capital was a freight train, but I could not afford to be choosy. I found a place for the potatoes and myself in one of the wagons, which at least was closed and, therefore, I wasn't completely exposed to the freezing cold. Unfortunately, this train's final destination was not Budapest. Approximately halfway there, I had to leave my closed wagon and search for connecting transportation. Luckily, I again managed to find a freight train heading to Budapest, but unfortunately this train only had open wagons.

I had no choice but to climb aboard. The train had just started to roll out of the station when it started to snow. It was cold and it was snowing. However, thanks to the wisdom of nature, when it snows, temperatures tend to rise. Therefore, the sub-zero temperature didn't kill me during the few hours until we arrived at the outskirts of Budapest, in a neighborhood which wasn't very far from Örömvölgy Street where we lived. So, when the train stopped near my destination, I jumped off with my sack of potatoes and dragged the potatoes and myself home. Edit and the others let me feel like a hero returning from the battlefield, which exactly reflected my feelings as well.

I have to mention here the surgery that I underwent in Budapest during the summer of 1945. The big toe on my right foot, which had frozen during the forced march in January 1945, had to be operated on. The surgery was performed in one of the larger hospitals in Budapest. It was very painful. The doctors extracted the toenail during the surgery. I felt as if the local anesthesia they had given me wasn't effective at all. Not only was the operation painful it also left my big toe distorted and out of shape to this very day.

The winter of 1945–46 was harsh, similar to that of 1944–45. At the end of December, with my day of departure fast approaching, I spent those last cold days in Budapest with Edit, little Vera, Vilmos, Edit's father and Juliska, her mother. At last, Vilmos also had a job, of a sort, with the Joint organization and as part of his first wages, he proudly brought home one single can of sardines. This treasure was carefully placed in the pantry should a real food supply emergency arise.

I've been thinking of Edit's state of mind when she consented to let me leave for *Eretz Yisrael*. How worried was she about me, about my future? Was she sorry that I was leaving or maybe relieved to be getting rid of the responsibility? Of course, those were not normal times. Just think about the anguish of the parents when boys and girls of my age and even younger asked for permission to start out for *Eretz Yisrael* through war-devastated Europe of 1945–46. But most parents I knew about, agreed. Thus on January 1, 1946, a group of us Jewish youth, boys and girls, were to meet in the so-called "South railroad station" in Buda to travel to Vienna.

Early in the morning of that important day in my life, I left the apartment on Örömvölgy Street never to return again. This was to prove not quite true, because in 1998, during one of my visits to Budapest, out of curiosity, I went to look at the building that by then was in near ruins.

On my shoulder that day in 1946 was a knapsack containing my clothes and some food that Edit had packed for me. I was warmly dressed with a winter coat and fur cap and set out for the tram station, crossing the only functioning bridge between Pest and Buda.

Arriving at the end of the tramline, which was on the Pest side of the Danube River, I met Misi for the first time. Misi, who later became my good friend, was a very original type of person. He was accompanied by his father who himself was a unique character. According to the legend that I later heard among the guys, our *hevre*, Mr. Ede Friedman, Misi's father, had introduced his son to the "facts of life" in a very original way. He supposedly accompanied Misi to the brothel on Konti Street in Budapest. I don't know whether this story is true or not, but Misi, very proudly, never denied it. He just let the rumor spread, never contradicting it.

Anyhow, on that cold and sunny morning of January 1, 1946, I didn't yet know anything about Misi besides the fact that he was also heading in the direction of Buda's South railroad station. So the three of us, Misi, his father and I crossed the temporary bridge (erected across the Danube after the original was destroyed during the siege of Budapest), on our way to our rendezvous. Among Misi's belongings, I observed his trumpet, which was later used (and abused) by him, Yona and Kuka. All of these guys were still strangers to me on that cold winter morning of January, but not for long.

When Misi, his father and I arrived at the station, the train that was to take us to Vienna was already waiting. Most of our group of Jewish youngsters was already there and had started to settle down inside the wagons.

REBORN

I was fifteen years and four months old when I boarded that train to Vienna. The third phase of my life was about to commence.

I am not exaggerating when I say that right after meeting the boys and girls with whom I was to travel, I felt that my life had changed to something good. I felt it right away, as if I had already arrived home. Maybe it was even more than this. I was elated as if I were born anew.

The boys in the carriage were from a group called *Hanita*. It was named after the kibbutz on the Lebanese border that symbolized *Homa uMigdal* (Wall and Tower), the heroic movement to settle in the midst of hostile Arab populations during the British Mandate in Palestine. The girls in the passenger car were from a group called *Hagshama* (Realization), signaling the most important duty of a Zionist, i.e., to make *Aliya*.

On the morning of January 1, 1946, the train pulled out of the station in Buda on its way to Vienna. We were instructed not to speak Hungarian—we were supposed to be Polish. Why? Don't ask me, but those were the ways of the *Bricha* (Escape) organization, which was the Zionist organization in charge of "smuggling people over the border", or helping Jews wanting to make *Aliya* to pass from country to country on their way to *Eretz Yisrael*, without proper legal papers.

A little while after the train started to move, a young man of about twenty plus, who introduced himself as Yussuf (same name as used by one in the *Hanita* group), informed us that he was going to be the *Madrich* or counselor of our *Eida* or group, which included the boys and girls I have mentioned, under a new name of *Af Al Pi Chen*, which translates as, "Yes, In Spite of It". This meant that we, our *Eida*, was determined to make *Aliya* to *Eretz Yisrael* in spite of the British White Paper, which limited Jewish immigration to Mandatory Palestine to only 1,500 persons per month.

While we were all sitting together, I was asked my Hebrew name. I said that my name was Asher. Yona, who as I later found out, in the summer of 1945 had given the name Sárkány (which translates as "dragon" in Hungarian) to my future wife, proclaimed that Asher was too formal. He proposed that I be called Ashi. And so it was that I became Ashi, which is my nickname to this day among my comrades from those early days. Nicknames stuck to all of us with such force that even the children of our comrades from those days called my late wife Sárkány although her proper name in Hebrew was Tova and Rózsika in Hungarian.

After introductions and name giving in the wagon, the time came to eat. It was only natural for a group, which was about to live in a collective community, to gather the food brought by each and share it all together. I was very happy with this arrangement considering the fact that I had in my knapsack a most meager supply of food. Others brought delicacies like butter, cheese and salami and plenty of good bread.

Volunteers among us prepared the food and distributed it. One of them was Sárkány who, as I later found out, was always among the workers pulling her own weight, even more than what was required and expected of her. Anyhow, she used to tease me even after we were long married that I was attracted to her because when we first started our long journey together on the train she was among those handling and handing out the food. I always enjoy eating, so I was doubly content on that day in the train traveling with this group to my homeland.

In retrospect, I have tried to analyze why I felt that way. Why was I so relieved to be leaving Hungary and be on my way to *Eretz Yisrael*? It is not easy to be honest in such an analysis. I am far from being certain that I can do this correctly, but I will try.

There is not much doubt in my mind that the main reason for my wishing to leave Hungary was the terrible recent past. The pain of losing my parents, of losing my uncle Öcsi whom I admired, was with me all the time and in a certain way is still part of me to this very day. So was the humiliation that I suffered by the experience of the concentration camp and its aftermath. Although I was and still am proud of the fact that I, all alone as a boy of fourteen, managed to survive that hell, without having committed any act for which I should feel ashamed.

I have often wondered in recent years what would have happened if the events of 1944 had turned out differently. Let's imagine for a moment that the Soviet army, which was anyhow already on the border of Hungary, had occupied Hungary and liberated the Jews before the Germans had had a chance to deport us to Auschwitz. Would my family have remained intact, i.e., survived? Would we have left for the Land of Israel or the United States or stayed in Hungary? What about the majority of Hungarian Jews, would they have left the country?

We know that the Jews of Romania immigrated to Israel despite the fact that a large number of them in the Romanian heartland were not really hurt by the Germans. Similarly, most of the Jews of Bulgaria immigrated to Israel after the war although they were protected by the gentile population during the war and thus came to no harm. Who knows how everything in our lives might have changed or maybe stayed the same?

But back to reality. Why did I decide in 1946 to leave Hungary and go to *Eretz Yisrael*? On the positive side of the coin was the pride of belonging to *Hashomer Hatzair*, of being part of the Zionist movement. It really felt as if I was on the top of the world. There was no doubt at all in my mind that I was doing the right thing, as was also the case with my comrades.

There were, however, additional reasons that prompted me to want to leave. I hadn't found my place with Aunt Edit. She was trying very hard but barely managed to keep her head above water. For sure, I must have been a burden on her and the rest of her family. I wasn't doing well enough in school in Budapest, whereas beforehand I had always been at the top of my class. I didn't have many friends either. Only when I joined a Zionist movement did I find a lot of friends, boy and girl friends. I was hungry; I was dreaming of eating oranges and pineapples in new the Land of Israel.

By the way, when I finally arrived successfully in *Eretz Yisrael*, I was disappointed to find out that although there were plenty of oranges, there were no pineapples. I had to wait maybe thirty years before I tasted an Israeli-grown pineapple and even then I found it sour, worse than the pineapple in tin cans.

♦

We arrived in Vienna in the late afternoon of that same day, January 1, 1946. Vienna was under the formal occupation of the Four Powers—the Soviet Union, the United States, Britain and France. However, I believe the Soviet influence was dominant. Our group, we must have been a little less than a hundred, ranging in age from ten to twenty, mounted an electric tram and headed towards the Rothschild hospital. It would be more correct to say that this building used to be a Jewish hospital—in the pre-Nazi era. When we arrived in 1946, it served as a gathering place for Jews arriving from Eastern Europe, mostly with the final destination of *Eretz Yisrael* in mind. We were given food there—unbelievable luxuries like Ovaltine, which was a kind of ersatz war-time cacao, chewing gum, chocolate, milk powder in tin cans, etc.

Then we went to sleep, boys and girls in separate chambers, but not before the first and maybe only physical confrontation, that I remember, between two youths of our group. It is really remarkable that during our long journey to Mandatory Palestine which followed, very seldom were there any blows exchanged among the boys or girls.

This confrontation in Vienna took place between Yona of *Af Al Pi Chen* and a youth called Mordi from the *Irgun Bli Pshara*. This *Irgun* (organization) was the group of the oldest boys and girls; *Af Al Pi Chen* came next. By the way *Bli Pshara* translates as 'No Compromise', supposedly referring to our right to make *Aliya* and to live in *Eretz Yisrael* with no outside interference. I am not sure anymore what the reason was for the fight between Yona and Mordi, which I think was broken up just before serious blows were exchanged and didn't last long. I think it had something to do with Heli, Yona's girlfriend, who lived in Vienna and whom Yona was determined to convince to join us on our way to the Land of Israel.

As we discovered later in Vienna, Yona met Heli and convinced her to run away from her parents' home, to travel with us to *Eretz Yisrael*. So a couple of days later, while boarding the train leaving Vienna, Heli was smuggled on board by Yona and some of his friends and hidden up in the baggage rack. Heli's desperate parents became aware that she had run away, and were frantically searching for her on the train. Heli was located in the baggage rack by the conductor and removed from the train. It was by sheer miracle that nobody from our group was arrested for kidnapping.

After this misadventure neither Yona nor anyone else ever heard from Heli. To my best knowledge, she never made *Aliya*. As I later also found out, Yona, who is my friend to this very day, was a fighter with an ambition to box. This he inherited from his uncle on his father's side, Imre Mandi, who was a boxer in his youth. Yona admired this uncle and even kept a picture of him boxing.

The next morning after our arrival in Vienna, I immediately noticed a boy from my group of *Af Al Pi Chen* busily doing something. It was Dov, crouching on the floor with a number of tin boxes in front of him. He was experimenting with various mixtures of milk powder. God knows for what purpose. Many, many years later, I became convinced that Dov was a born cook who mistakenly became an aircraft mechanic instead of pursuing the career of a great chef.

Later in the morning, a *Misdar*, or assembly, was held. We all lined up in rows and columns, military fashion, and then Moshe Weis addressed us in Hungarian. Moshe originated from a little village in the vicinity of the place where I was born. He told us that we now belonged to *Ken Hatchia* which literally means "Nest of the Rebirth", and that we would be traveling through Germany on our way to Mandatory Palestine. Almost every day after that, there was a *Misdar* held by Moshe, in which he always started with the words *kodem kol*, "before anything else".

We stayed a couple of days in Vienna. We even went to the swimming pool and also to the theater to see the operetta *Martha*, which was Central Europe's version of an American musical. One should keep in mind that in their own view, Hungary and most certainly Austria belong to Central, and not Eastern, Europe.

Then we were off, again by train to a large ex-military camp in a little town by the name of Kleinmünchen. The camp consisted of several subdivisions, one of them a prison for hundreds of German prisoners of war. We only stayed one night there and then traveled to Salzburg where we were lodged on the outskirts of town in a beautiful castle apparently abandoned by its owners but still in good condition. I was particularly impressed in Salzburg by the public transportation, which was based on electric trolleys. These were electric trams, but instead of rails like all the trams I had seen before, traveled on tires, just like buses.

After Salzburg, we traveled to Ainring in Germany just across the Austrian border. There, we slept in the barracks of a former German Luftwaffe base. They still had military aircraft sitting in the hangars. We spent some of our spare time in and out of the cockpit of a Junker fighter.

In Airing, I chose my first "post-Hungary" girlfriend by the name of Anna. She was a quiet girl with pretty rosy cheeks. Anna wasn't among the founders of *Af Al Pi Chen* a few days before, but I convinced her and our leaders to let her join our group. At the same time, I also met and befriended Kerami who belonged to Anna's group and convinced her to also join *Af Al Pi*. Since I was in the convincing mode, I persuaded another two girls, Rachel and Havi, to also join *Af Al Pi*. So now at least we had plenty of girls in our group. I am not sure though that our "original" girls were very enthusiastic about the results of my efforts.

Ainring is not far away from Bad Reichenhall, which is a fashionable place for a summer or winter vacation, surrounded by wonderful mountains with plenty of deep-water lakes in the vicinity. We also visited Berchtesgaden, a small village in the same general area. It became infamous by the fact that Hitler had his favorite retreat, the Eagle's Nest, in those mountains. It was presented to Hitler by his loyal followers and was a fortress-like facility located on one of the mountain peeks.

Our group decided to visit these places. We climbed by foot the snow-covered road leading to Hitler's villa which was quite intact. It looked like a place where people had been living recently. Then, in January 1946 we were the only visitors there. Nowadays, although there is not much public information about the place, it is swarming with visitors; bus after bus of tourists comes and goes. In 1946, we at least managed to do some damage, breaking the glass surrounding the main balcony of the villa. In later years, the villa itself was completely demolished and presently only the underground bunkers of Hitler's command center exist. In January 1946, we couldn't reach the

Eagle's Nest itself because one can get there only by special transportation along a steep road.

Judith and I did travel there in August 1999. The final stage of reaching the fortress's upper platform has to be accomplished by a specially installed elevator which nowadays serves the many visitors who want to observe for themselves where he, the Monster or the Führer, depending on one's point of view, functioned. Anyhow, we were in high spirits after our trip there in January 1946, most probably because we were young and felt that we were alive, on our way to a new life and he who wanted to destroy us all is rotting somewhere under the ruins of his Berlin headquarters.

After a couple more days in Ainring, on a sunny and chilly morning on January 17, 1946, a number of US army trucks arrived and we boarded them to travel to our final destination in Strüth bei Ansbach. We traveled all day and arrived at Strüth in late afternoon. Just as in Vienna, we were given a first class late lunch or early dinner and we were happy.

This beautifully located place, not too far from Nuremberg, which in the past held a sanitarium for patients with lung disease, during the war was an SS convalescing center. It is located a couple of kilometers away from the medium-sized town of Ansbach. In front of the sanitarium there is a green field and behind it, a forest. It is a lovely place and this was to be our home for some eighteen months.

In Strüth, we found another group of *Hashomer Hatzair* youngsters, which had departed from Budapest several weeks before. They had first traveled to Prague, arriving in Strüth several days before us. This group consisted of Hungarian and Polish Jewish children. The person in charge of the Polish children was Dr. Kotarba (Kotarba was his *nom de guerre*, his real name was Dr. Osterweil but everyone called him Kotarba). Kotarba was a well-built, not too tall man, in his forties. He was an old-time *Hashomer Hatzair* member from Poland. The Hungarian children were organized in a group called *Dor Hadash* (New Generation), with the person in charge being Ervin Birnbaum, a young man about seventeen or eighteen years old who was born in Kassa. I suppose that when the group left Hungary, the Hungarians and Poles were all together and Kotarba was in charge of the entire group. Some conflict along the way must have caused this split into Hungarian and Polish sub-groups. With my own group's arrival in Strüth, *Dor Hadash* immediately became part of our *Ken Hatchia* but Kotarba's children were organized separately although we all lived together in the same building for many months to come. In the summer of 1946, a third group of Hungarian children arrived from Budapest and they also became part of *Ken Hatchia*.

Ervin Birnbaum was greatly admired by the youngsters in *Dor Hadash* and respected by all. It was, therefore, a great shock to everyone when, later in 1947 after the Exodus voyage (a heroic adventure, which I will recount as we proceed), he disappeared. Ervin returned to Kassa and later sent us a letter explaining the reason for abandoning us. He explained that although he had described the relationship between his father and mother in ideal terms, the sad reality was different. In his letter, he claimed that he had had to return to Kassa to try to straighten out things between his parents. Later, we found out that Ervin couldn't save his parents' marriage and they eventually divorced. I believed his story then and still believe it today. I also believe that he was suffering from pangs of conscience because he had deserted "his children" who so much believed in him. He told us in his letters that he would sit with a magnifying glass in front of photographs from Strüth, looking at the faces of the children he had left behind.

From Kassa, Ervin and his parents immigrated to New York, where he became a Conservative rabbi. He made *Aliya* to Israel with his wife and sons after the Six Day War. Before that, in the spring of 1967, I visited him in his Brooklyn home and was pleasantly surprised to see that his children and wife spoke fluent Hebrew and the regular notes on his refrigerator were written not in English, but in Hebrew.

When they made *Aliya*, the Birnbaum family first stayed in Kfar Habad from where I fetched them to visit us in our home in Rimon, Kiryat Ono. Because of the orthodox monopoly in Israel, he couldn't practice as a (Conservative) rabbi. Ervin, therefore, moved with his family to Sde Boker, where he made his living by teaching English in the seminar there. We visited them at Sdeh Boker a number of times, but later on lost contact. The last time I heard from him directly was when he phoned to condole me after my wife, Sárkány, passed away and then later I heard him by chance on the radio speaking in Hungarian about his visits to Budapest and his religious activities there.

I mentioned the kind of relationship which existed or actually didn't exist between the two *Hashomer Hatzair* groups in Strüth, one Hungarian and the other Polish. It is really amazing how it came about. Youngsters of a similar age, living in the same building, all from the same Zionist movement, having the same ideological background and the same goals in life, barely spoke to each other. There wasn't even a real language barrier because most of the Polish kids spoke Hungarian, which most of them had acquired while hiding in Hungary during the war.

In our group, we, of course, spoke Hungarian among ourselves. There were only a few kids who spoke Yiddish and even less who spoke Hebrew, mostly a handful who had gone to one of the two Hebrew language schools in either Uzhgorod (in prewar Czechoslovakia; Ungvar, Hungary, during the war; in Ukraine today) or Mukačevo (Munkács), like my spouse, Judith.

There was also an additional strange situation in Strüth. Besides the youth belonging to *Hashomer Hatzair*, there were some other Hungarian youngsters of similar age from a different Zionist movement, the *Dror Habonim*. This movement was not as far left on the political scale as *Hashomer Hatzair*, but was close enough. It is hard to explain why there was hardly any social contact between these two groups of Hungarian Jewish kids. Such separation was even more unnatural if one considers that there were even boys and girls from the same school in Hungary, maybe even from the same class, but in Strüth they were like strangers to each other.

The only common institutions for these two groups were the infirmary and the school, which were set up soon after our arrival in Strüth in a few of the smaller buildings. The Polish children, as far as I remember, didn't attend the school but they used the infirmary. Food was served separately for the three groups; Hungarian *Hashomer Hatzair* and *Dror Habonim*, and Polish *Hashomer Hatzair*.

After the arrival of the third Hungarian *Hashomer Hatzair* group, the quality and quantity of the food we were given started to deteriorate. During our first months in Strüth both the quality and quantity of food were excellent. However, this situation didn't last long. After a while, we started to go hungry. When one is hungry, really hungry, as we were, one doesn't bother much about the quality of the food. Quantity becomes the only issue. Things were getting worse and worse, especially for the teenagers who were at the age when one needs a lot of food. Thus, whenever we walked to the nearby town of Ansbach, we looked for, collected and ate beets, which were growing in the fields adjacent to the road.

I could never comprehend, and still don't understand, why there wasn't enough food for our group, especially since the Polish group didn't go hungry.

The situation deteriorated so much that there were instances when some of us begged for food from the kitchen of the Polish group.

To the best of my knowledge, the *Dror Habonim* group also didn't go hungry. What was the reason for this lack of provisions only for our, even though the largest, group? Was it bad housekeeping, was someone stealing our food supply? I have no proper explanation but the fact is that for maybe over a year we were continually hungry.

In one of the first days after our arrival in Strüth, Yussuf, the *Madrich* of *Af Al Pi*, led us all into the forest. We picked a beautiful spot to congregate and seated ourselves around Yussuf. This place was to be our *Sela Hamoatza*, our "Rock of Assembly". Yussuf opened the conversation by telling us to imagine that we were all involved in a shipwreck and that there was only one place left in the lifeboat for our group. Who should be allowed to take that single life-saving spot? Yussuf called upon everyone to argue on his own behalf. "Why should I be the one saved?" was the question each of us was challenged to answer.

I forgot what argument I brought up on my behalf. I remember though that it was quite silly. I have also forgotten all the other arguments except what Rafi said for himself because it was so... bizarre. Rafi tried to convince us that he should be saved because he had an uncle in America and Rafi wanted to meet this uncle, whom he had never seen. I am not sure that I even believed at the time that Rafi really had an uncle in the U.S., but I was astonished by the sheer peculiarity of his argument.

Well, it turned out later that, yes, this uncle in the U.S. really existed and we all met him in Israel in 1967 after the Six Day War. The uncle was called Marton and we became good friends. He visited us in Israel and I visited him several times in the U.S. Marton was a bachelor all his life; he had a brother and sister in the U.S. in addition to Rafi's mother, who was his sister. Marton finally married Sari whom I also met and liked, but he fell sick and passed away several years ago in Miami. So Rafi at the "Rock of Assembly" in Strüth wasn't bluffing.

Yussuf, our *Madrich*, was some years older. In Budapest, he had studied to become a teacher and he was, and still is, a dedicated teacher and leader of the young. We liked him a lot, I especially so. At the beginning of 1947, he left with a group of the youngest children to Hamburg-Blankensee where they all waited for their turn to travel to *Eretz Yisrael*.

There was a young woman in that town, a *Shaliach*, or emissary, from the Jewish Agency, by the name of Reuma Schwartz. Later in Israel, Reuma married Ezer Weizman, the legendary Commander of the Israeli Air Force who then became President of Israel. Reuma's older sister, Ruth, became the wife of the even more legendary Moshe Dayan who was Chief of Staff of the Israeli Defense Forces (IDF) and became Minister of Defense just before the Six Day War in 1967, only to resign in shame after the Yom Kippur War of 1973. When in the mid-seventies, Menachem Begin became Prime Minister, Dayan became his Foreign Minister and very much succeeded in purging himself from his unfortunate role in the Yom Kippur War by his leading role in the peace process with Egypt.

In Blankensee, Yussuf and Reuma became good friends. Among other stories, Reuma told him about her family's Arab friends in Jerusalem; the first shots in the Arab uprising that began in 1936 were fired on their home from the very direction of the house of those same friends.

As I have said, I liked Yussuf a lot and was excited when a few days after our arrival in Strüth he summoned me one morning. He explained that now that there were more children with us, a reorganization had to take place. A number of the younger boys would constitute a new group and Yussuf wanted me to be their *Madrich*. It was a great honor for me especially because I was a newcomer, who only a couple of weeks before had joined this bunch of youngsters. I gladly accepted his proposal and thus became the *Madrich* of boys aged thirteen to foureen. My *Kvutza,* or group, was named *Magshimim,* or Implementers (of the goals of Zionism).

The boys were: Zuki Zucherman, Benö Benedek, Pityu Münz, Döcse Deutsch, Yoel Feldmann, Gyuri Wax, Csuti and later, Gyuri Schlesinger.

Zuki was his family's youngest son; he was born when his father was in his late sixties, maybe even early seventies. He was a delicated, gifted, intelligent, sensitive boy. Unfortunately, after his service in the army and in his early years at the university in Jerusalem he became disillusioned with the realities of life in Israel and emigrated, ending up in France. He is married with children and lives in Paris, where he makes his living in real estate, but for fun, translates Hungarian literature into French.

Benö was my future and now late wife's younger brother who just like his sister tragically passed away some years ago. Benö, like Zuki, started out in Kibbutz Kfar Masaryk, but left the kibbutz quite early on and became a sports reporter for the Yediot Ahronot daily newspaper. He is survived by his wife, Zvia, a gifted writer of children's stories, and by two wonderful children, Amir his son who has a doctorate in physics and a lovely daughter named Orit. Amir is father to a six-year-old daughter and Orit is mother to three sons.

Pityu was a hyperactive boy, a pretty boy and I believe also gifted. He had a sister in one of the girls' groups and later their mother also passed through Strüth. I lost touch with Pityu after our 1948 arrival in the Land of Israel, but heard rumors in later years that he worked as a waiter on a ship and that he was involved in some sort of a stabbing incident over his girlfriend. Benö, who recounted this occurrence to me years later, also told me that Pityu promised to knife me as well, if and when we would meet.

"Why did he want to punish or even kill me?" I asked Benö. Well, according to Pityu, I was responsible for ruining his life. "How did I ruin his life?" I asked. Well, after our final arrival in Mandatory Palestine in the spring of 1948, some of the boys from my group were sent to Kibbutz Kfar Masaryk, but not all of them. Pityu wasn't. He was sent to an educational center near Netanya. Pityu felt that had he been sent to Kfar Masaryk, he would have been more successful in life. Maybe yes; maybe no; I doubt it. It is my firm conviction that success or failure in life, provided one is healthy and lives in a free society (like Israel), is completely up to the person himself. So, if Pityu felt that he hadn't fulfilled his aspirations, he should have looked for the reasons in his own heart.

Anyhow, one thing is certain. When we arrived, I had no influence over who was sent where. In the spring of 1948, I didn't even speak Hebrew and when these boys and girls were selected to be taken to this or that kibbutz or to one of the educational centers, nobody even bothered to ask my opinion or waited for my recommendation. At any rate, after a certain age every grown-up is responsible for his own fate. It is an easy way to escape responsibility by blaming one's failure on parents, educators or friends, more so if one lives in a free society.

To be completely honest, I also have to admit that in *Magshimim*, Zuki and Benö, who were good friends, were also the "stars" of the group and they knew it. When Gyuri Schlesinger arrived, he and Pityu became good friends but they were somewhat "on the outs". So the reason that Pityu as a grown-up talked about vengeance by stabbing me, most probably had its roots in the jealousy he must have felt in *Magshimim* towards Zuki and Benö, whom he saw as the favorites.

Döcse was born somewhere in central or western Hungary. According to the story I heard, his mother abandoned him as a baby and Döcse, or Joseph Deutsch, was raised as an orphan. Döcse was a good-hearted, not too sophisticated boy, eager to help, who, besides some very rare outbursts of irrational anger, had no quarrel with anyone. Some years ago, I heard that his mother, after many years of virtually no contact, showed up in Kfar Masaryk, where she remained to live with the son she had abandoned as a baby.

Yoel Feldmann, or "little" Yoel (so called because of his size), was a shrewd boy. He came from Debrecen and was among the "lucky" group of Jews of that town who were not deported to Auschwitz but to a slave labor camp near Vienna. There, the families were not separated and there were no gas chambers, and so Yoel and his whole family survived the war. His older brother, Zvi, later joined us with his wife and their little daughter who, according to her mother, was born in Auschwitz. Yes, a baby born in Auschwitz! This girl may have been the only Jewish baby who was born in Auschwitz and by some unexplained miracle was left alive. Yoel worked for many years in the Weizmann Institute in Rehovot, but I never met him again after our arrival in the Land of Israel.

Gyuri Wax was an only child. Since I was also an only child, I knew the symptoms, which are not always so good. We, the boys of *Magshimim* and I, all slept together in the same room. There were two floors to accommodate us. It was my duty as the *Madrich* to wake everyone in the morning. I often had a problem getting Gyuri Wax out of bed. He was a little lazy. Once, I couldn't convince him to get up and had to turn him out of bed. He didn't resist; Gyuri was a little phlegmatic and seldom smiled. I had no contact with him after our arrival, although I know that after his service in the IDF, he became a police officer and lived in Haifa. It turned out that Gyuri was a first cousin to Ági (she wasn't with us in Strüth), who became Yona's wife. Ági told me some years ago that Gyuri Wax had passed away.

Csuti was a silent and completely passive boy. He spoke very seldom and had a bashful smile when spoken to. Csuti's only real contact in Strüth was with Seren, his sister. Seren was in a girls' group where Sárkány was the *Madricha*. If I am not mistaken, Csuti and Seren were twins. In our *Magshimim* group only Benö had some meaningful, though limited, communication with Csuti. So I never knew what was going on in his mind.

To our great surprise when our time came to leave Strüth in June 1947 for *Eretz Yisrael*, Csuti announced that he wasn't going with us. There was no changing his mind. Csuti had decided to immigrate to the United States. He left us then and there. Many years later, I heard from someone who met Seren in Rehovot that Csuti had made it to the U.S. and was still living there.

Gyuri Schlesinger arrived in Strüth in the spring or summer of 1946 with his mother and older brother. He was a nice-looking, gifted boy with a sardonic sense of humor. He spoke some English, which was quite unusual among the crowd in Strüth. In Israel, I met him in the Air Force where he at first learned to be a mechanic and later trained and became a fighter pilot. He was among the few pilots whose Spitfire was shot down by the Egyptians in the Sinai War of 1956; he was only twenty five years old. After his death, his mother and brother immigrated to Australia.

The social fiber connecting all of us in Strüth was unbelievably strong. Loyalty to the group was the strongest loyalty most of us had. It was even stronger than the loyalty to one's family, which was the reason why good children like Sárkány and Dov ran away from home—Sárkány from her mother and Dov from his father, mother, brother and sister.

The Rosenberg sisters illustrate this binding force. These were two thirteen- and fourteen-year-old girls who came from a religious family. Of course, *Hashomer Hatzair* was anything but religious. These sisters were with us in Strüth when, in our first few weeks there, their mother suddenly appeared. She came to take away her daughters. Apparently, the Rosenberg family was quite wealthy because after the war they were able to settle in Switzerland. The mother told the daughters what a good life and the best education they were going to have in Switzerland in one of the most prestigious Jewish boarding schools for the very rich. She couldn't convince them to leave. Eventually she had to remove them from Strüth by force and thus took them with her to the "exile" of Switzerland.

When the sisters left it was like witnessing a great tragedy unfolding before our eyes. Everyone felt the sorrow of these two young girls. It was as if a close family member suddenly had to leave the tribe for some tragic reason.

♦

The first year in Strüth was fun. A grade school with nine levels was set up for the children. The lectures were in Hungarian, but, among the subjects taught, the Hebrew language occupied an important slot.

A good part of the children's lives was spent in group activities for which the *Madrichim* like me were responsible. I gave presentations on Zionism, biology, world history, etc. We had heated discussions on many subjects, including the policies of the British Mandate in Palestine, Socialism, the Soviet Union, etc. Scouting activities were important, as were different kinds of sports like volleyball and football.

Every Friday evening there was an *Oneg Shabbat*, a party celebrating the Sabbath. Each group had the responsibility to prepare a program for those occasions. My group of *Magshimim* was very good at preparing and presenting theater pieces. We wrote the story, prepared the costumes, erected the stage settings, including the lights and curtains, and, of course, the boys were the actors in the various roles. Some of these presentations weren't half bad. Such an activity was followed by dancing. No ballroom-type dances like the fox trot or tango were allowed. Not that anyone formally prohibited them, but they were never on the agenda; such dances were considered bourgeois. Only folk dances were in vogue, including the *Hora* and one special *Hora* in which four boys formed a circle, each grabbing the belt of the two next to him and furiously gyrating at ever-increasing speed. The most popular dance however was the *Bein Haharim* or "Between the Mountains" in which all present formed a large circle chanting *Bein Haharim Tisa Harakevet...*, "Between the Mountains the Train Travels...", while a boy or a girl danced around inside the circle and then selected another partner to dance with. When a boy or girl thus selected was believed to be her or his "date", the chanting turned into a loud shouting of "Oho, oho, oho...", which most probably indicated recognition by the group of the pair's official couple-status. Yes, a number of couples were formed among the boys and girls, but contrary to the liberal morality from the 1960s to the present era, the sexual behavior of the couples in Strüth was very conservative. Hand touching, kissing, caressing accompanied by some very intensive talking were the limit.

Among us were young women and men, fifteen to twenty years old and constantly together and I don't know of even a single pregnancy during the more than two-year period in which we were together, first in Strüth and later during our journey to *Eretz Yisrael*. Although boys and girls slept in separate rooms, the day-to-day relationships were without any formal restrictions. Equality between the sexes was the rule of the day, however limited by the terms and standards of those days. For instance, conventional "feminine" tasks like laundry were performed by girls only.

There was no real "grown-up" supervision at all. The leader of *Ken Hatchia*, Moshe Weis, was hardly more than twenty three or at most twenty five years old. At the beginning, he and his wife Tamar were the only married couple in Strüth. Later, by the end of 1946 or beginning of 1947, some two or three young married couples, from the outside world, joined *Ken Hatchia*, as well.

So how can one explain the very subdued sexual activity in Strüth? There certainly weren't any written or verbal rules regulating it. Nobody forbade anything; I don't even remember if the subject ever came up in the educational forum of the *Madrichim* of which I was a member and always participated in its meetings. I think that moral "purity" which, among other more specific ideologies, directs vanguard movements and *Hashomer Hatzair* proudly claimed such vanguard status, coupled with bourgeois morality, which middle-class Hungarian children like us acquired at home, was responsible for this self-restricting behavior. Anyhow, I also had girlfriends in Strüth: first, with Anna for a very short time, followed by Rita and then Sárkány, later again Rita and then again Sárkány.

Rita was a very gifted person, with red, rather, bronze-colored hair. She was born on board a ship in the harbor of Rio de Janeiro on December 31, 1931. She had shining, teasing, smiling eyes. The romantic timing and place of her birth was significant in forming her personality. As a teenager, and then for her entire adult life, she claimed to be in love with Ervin Birnbaum, feelings which didn't interfere with her two marriages, first in Israel and later in the US. Rita arrived in *Eretz Yisrael* in the summer of 1947 before all of us. When on board the British prison ship Empire Rival in the bay of Marseilles (which story I will relate later), one of the younger girls suffered an acute attack of appendicitis and Rita was designated to disembark and take her to the hospital.

After the sick girl recovered, they were both allowed to travel to Mandatory Palestine and Rita was sent to Kibbutz Negba. There she met her future husband and they had two children, a boy and a girl. The couple and children had a harsh life in Israel and later tried their luck in Germany, the country Rita's husband originated from, with very little success. They returned to Israel and later divorced. A couple of years later, Rita married an American Jew, originally from Poland, and settled down in the Queens borough of New York. This man adored her and, although she liked him, she was much above him intellectually. He was always telling me how we, Rita's friends, should be ashamed because we didn't properly care for "such a jewel", as he lovingly described Rita. I visited them a couple of times in their Queens home, first in 1967 and then in the 1970s. Rita's rhapsodic nature didn't allow her to be "boxed" into the middle class neighborhood of Queens. In addition, her children lived in Israel so she often flew between New York and Tel Aviv. She always wanted to learn to drive and tragically met her death in Israel in a car accident on the highway near Ashkelon while taking a driving lesson.

Other couples among my friends were Dov-Zseni, Rafi-Tamar, Misi-Hava, Yona-Amalia, and sometimes Yona-Lilien. The majority of the children were orphans—most had lost their parents during the war.

There were a number of siblings among us: Sárkány and her younger brother Avri; Tomi or Benoe (based on his last name of Benedek); Judith or Macko (given this name because she wore an overall called a *macko*) and her younger brother Tomi or Zvi (Tomi was in Strüth for only a short while because his mother came and took him back to a small town in Czechoslovakia); Seren and her younger brother Csuti; Anna and her younger brother nicknamed Kis Diszno or "Piggy"; Lilien and her younger brother Dudi; Icu and his younger brother Tubica (his older brother liked to pamper him); Kalman and his sister Eva; Miriam and her younger sister Erzsi; the twins, Sanyi and Tibi, who survived Mengele's "medical" experiments in Auschwitz; Gyuri Schlesinger and his older brother Shmuel; the Herman family (Sanyi and his younger brother Putyuli and their two sisters, Kisanya and the younger Kis-Kisanya, both of them beautiful girls); Dagi and her younger brother Peter (born in Vienna, Austria, to a Jewish mother and non-Jewish father who later served in the German Army during the war); Partizan (nicknamed because he had a partisan cap) and his younger sister Siami (nicknamed because her face resembled that of a Siamese cat); Kobi (because he looked very Jewish) and his younger sister Mongol (because she had a Far Eastern complexion); Zvi Feldmann and his younger brother Yoel; Nagy (or Big) Tutu and his younger brother Kis (or Little) Tutu; Pityu Muenz and his younger sister Klari; Endre Baron and his younger brother Tomi; Meir Perl and his younger sister Malka. Among the not so young were Yamoy Holländer and his younger sister Irma.

Tamar Schiff was also in Strüth with her husband, Joseph, and younger brother, Moshe. When later, in June 1947, we were boarding our *Aliya Bet* ship, the S.S. Exodus, the Schiff couple was so terrified at the sight of this shaky vessel that they demanded (and achieved) that Moshe, who was already on the ship, disembark. At the time, this was considered to be an act of "desertion" though from the perspective of over fifty years, things seem different now. As far as I know, the Schiff couple and Moshe remained in France and have maybe lived there ever since.

◆

Our life in Strüth was in complete isolation from the outside world, as if we were living on an island. Although geographically we were located near Nuremberg in the midst of post-war Western Germany occupied by the American Army, there was very little contact with either the local German population or the occupying American forces. Yes, from time to time we went to the cinema in nearby Ansbach, and sometimes even managed to eat *Kartoffel Salat*, potato salad, and drink *Bier mit Schuss*, beer with some sweet juice, in one of the local restaurants. But these were the only encounters we had with the Germans, besides working in Strüth with the gardener and the obviously antisemitic boiler attendant.

We had even less contact with the American occupying forces. We saw their soldiers in Ansbach. For many years to come there was an American military base nearby with soldiers on leave and military police circulating the town. Our food supply was from UNRRA, which used American army vehicles driven by soldiers, some of them Afro-American, which in itself was a new phenomenon for us, having only ever seen Afro-Americans in the movies.

We were enclosed in our own little and very idealistic world—thinking of *Aliya* and talking about Zionism and Socialism most of the time. We were so naive and absolutely certain in our ideology that I remember myself once leading a discussion with the boys in my *Magshimim* group explaining my conviction that surely even Winston Churchill must know in the depths of his mind that Socialism, like that practiced then in the Soviet Union, is the future and the only right way for all humanity.

Even though we were hungry, we had a wonderful time, especially during the first nine months in Strüth. Then two of our groups—*Irgun Bli*

Pshara, containing the older of the young men and women on their way to Mandatory Palestine, and the group of the youngest children accompanied by our *Madrich*, Yussuf, moved to Blankensee near Hamburg where the center was judged to be more suitable for younger children.

Our daily routine was interrupted in the early spring of 1947 when some thirty or so of my friends went to work for a few weeks in Triesdorf, as a sort of *Hachshara* or preparation for our future life in a Kibbutz. In Triesdorf there was a sort of model German farm. Since I was in charge of a group of smaller children, I didn't travel right away with my colleagues to Triesdorf, but still managed to go there later, for a couple of days.

I have to admit that never before and maybe never after, did I observe such precise and meticulous organization of labor, nor did I freely work so hard at physical labor as there, on that farm. We woke early in the morning and, after a quick coffee or tea, gathered in the courtyard for the daily distribution of work assignments. I was to work in the forest cutting trees. Our group was given a certain quantity of trees to fell and then chop. The German in charge was so knowledgeable in his profession that the work allocated to us for the day was of such magnitude that, with ten hours of hard work, we just about managed to finish our task.

For all the others, whether they worked in agriculture or with the livestock, it was the same. All of us worked very, very hard. When, after finally eating our evening meal, the main ingredient of which was boiled potatoes, we got to bed. We were so tired that everyone fell asleep immediately without the usual jokes and laughter, which are typical when young people sleep in the same room.

ABOARD THE S.S. EXODUS

It was now close to eighteen months since our arrival in Strüth, waiting for our turn to make *Aliya*. Our patience was running out with the Jewish Agency, headquartered in Munich. Nobody knew why it was keeping us in Germany for such a long time. Was it because we were a Hungarian group and therefore discriminated against? After all, the men in charge in Munich were mostly from Poland and not from Hungary. Was there a communication problem because of language? Hungarians usually don't speak any language besides

Hungarian. Maybe the discrimination against us was political; because we were *Hashomer Hatzair* and in Munich the tone was set by the more mainstream Socialist Mapai Party. It is also possible that we were being kept in readiness to form an exceptionally large group of *Maapilim*, the name for those going to Mandatory Palestine illegally, as far as the British authorities were concerned, which was being assembled for the ship the Exodus. We didn't know anything. We knew though that we had been waiting long enough for our turn to be taken to *Eretz Yisrael*.

And then the day came. In early June 1947, without any prior notice, we were notified to prepare to leave at once in the direction of France. Everyone's morale suddenly peaked sky high and our whole group got ready to go. Everyone, that is, besides Csuti who, as I mentioned before, left us for the USA.

On June 29, 1947, the long forgotten UNRRA trucks arrived again—we boarded and left for Stuttgart. From there, we left by train for Strasbourg in France. Crossing into France was amazing. In Germany, most of the cities were in ruins, with destruction all around. Everywhere one could sense the depressed atmosphere among the population. Strasbourg was different. There were flowers in the windows and people were smiling. So we were also happy. Not that we had felt sorry for the Germans, of course, just the opposite. It was good to see the more or less normal life of the French.

After a very tiring train journey south we had to switch to trucks. Not all in our group were intended for the same camp because of lack of space and, therefore, it happened that one truckload of children was separated from the others. Rita and I were in charge of the children in that truck and we were directed to a beautiful little camp with a wonderful view of the Mediterranean Sea. I will never forget our first glance at the sea. Hungary has no border on any sea and in Strüth, Germany, we were also "land-locked". It was amazing, the vastness of water, which we observed for the first time in our lives.

We stayed in that camp for only a day or two and then on July 10, 1947, we were off for the ship that was to take us home to *Eretz Yisrael*. That morning, a number of trucks arrived to transport us to the harbor of Sete where the ship was waiting for us. We didn't know it at first, but found out soon enough, that this small vessel, originally designed for river cruises of 300, maybe 400 passengers, was to take all of our 4,530 passengers on a Mediterranean Sea voyage to Mandatory Palestine.

After more than fifty-five years, I am still flabbergasted and amazed at the organizational efficiency it took to embark such a large number of people in a very short period of time—not more than an hour!! Just consider that the men in charge of this operation had to arrange for at least 150 truckloads to carry over 4,500 men, women and children from different camps located in the general area of Marseilles into the harbor of Sete. I assume that many of the trucks had to travel more than once because surely the organizers didn't have 150 trucks. The trucks had to be loaded with people and their meager belongings at the camps and unloaded at the harbor. The telephone connection must have been terrible, remember this was 1947 when there were no commercially operated mobile phones yet, regular civilian telephone service was almost non-existent and the cooperation of the French authorities was so-so.

Embarking was via a single two-meter long plank connecting the quay with the ship. There were two "sailors" loudly helping and urging the thousands to board the ship as fast as possible. Once inside, other members of the crew directed each of us to his or her place. Not that it was much. Every individual was given a thirty or forty-centimeter wide and two-meter long space on a wooden two-decker bunk, (not unlike the ones I remembered from Jaworznow), which was to serve as bed, storage area and everything else for the whole journey.

It was during this very efficient embarkation process that we heard the Schiff family on the public address system, obviously horrified by the conditions existing on the boat, requesting their little Moshe to disembark, which he did as I mentioned above. I have never seen or heard of any of the Schiffs again.

Because the boat was built for far fewer passengers and different sailing conditions, it had to be reinforced. This was achieved by the use of thick wooden boards placed every few meters between the floor and the ceiling. To tell the truth, it was all very frightening. From a normal "civil" point of view, it was also irresponsible on the part of the organizers to so endanger 4,530 young people who had no way of resisting or even comprehending the dangers of the voyage they were about to undertake. But those were different, non-civil times. We were about to make history and were neither knowledgeable of nor troubled by the dangers ahead.

The Captain of the ship was called Ike, twenty or at most twenty five years old, who looked even younger with his rosy cheeks and whom we learned to much admire during our journey. However, the commander in charge of the operation on behalf of the Jewish Agency and the *Haganah* military organization was Yosef Harel (Hamburger), who was also on board, although his identity was unknown to us at the time.

The French authorities knew who the passengers of the ship were and its destination. They realized that the ship and its passengers were heading to Mandatory Palestine and they were familiar with the policy of His Majesty's Government in London, according to which such a sea voyage was illegal as defined in the British Government's White Paper. Still, the French were willing to close an eye and let the ship depart. However, Mr. Bevin, the notorious anti-Zionist UK Foreign Minister at the time, wasn't ready to give in. Via diplomatic channels, he demanded that our ship be forbidden to leave the port. The French complied and ordered our ship not to sail. According to international naval regulations, not only do all ships wishing to leave a harbor have to have a permit, it is also necessary that a pilot who knows the harbor board the ship to guide it to the open sea. Needless to say, when the French forbade our ship to leave port, they also gave orders to ensure that the pilot on duty wouldn't guide us out of our place of anchor.

The men in charge of our ship had a very difficult decision to make—whether to comply with the French decision and stay in Sete or disobey and risk sailing out of the harbor without a local pilot. Following a brief telephone consultation with the Jewish Agency's Paris office, the decision was taken to sail anyhow.

I happened to be on the deck when our boat started to move. It was already the night of July 11, 1947, three hours after midnight when the ship's engines were started and we moved out of the harbor. However, after a very short while, I heard a loud scratching sort of sound and the ship stopped. We had the bad luck of landing on a reef. The boat couldn't move. It was, of course, just to avoid such a situation that a pilot familiar with the location of the reefs has to guide ships leaving or entering any harbor in the world. Well, we were stranded and the situation looked grim. That was the first time I laid my eyes on our captain Yitzchak Aharonovitz or Ike. He looked so young that I first mistook him for one of the young passengers like myself. However, his firm, loud and authoritative voice, and the way it was immediately obeyed by the other crew members, didn't leave room for any misunderstanding—this young man was the captain of our ship. Ike ordered all engine throttles into full power again and again. Still the ship wouldn't move. Then suddenly, after numerous attempts, as if by miracle, the boat slowly started to move as it descended from its stranded position on the reef. It really was a miracle. The ship's bow could have been badly bruised, but it wasn't. The engines could have been damaged, but they weren't. The propellers could have been ruined, but they weren't. No serious damage to the ship was observed. After a few minutes we were out of the harbor and approaching the open sea on our way to the land of our dreams, to *Eretz Yisrael*.

Next morning, as we were slowly sailing towards our destination, we noticed a British military aircraft circling in the air around our ship. It was evident that we had been detected and it was obvious that the British government wasn't about to give up and allow us to safely land on the shores of "their" Palestine.

As we later found out, the *Haganah*'s plan was for our ship to reach the coast near Netanya, approach the shore as much as possible, then stretch ropes between our ship and the land and have the passengers get to the shore guided by these ropes. It sounds crazy? Yes, it was a crazy idea, but it had been successfully tried before with much smaller ships. I am not sure, however, that anyone really believed it possible to transport in such a manner 4,530 people, among them babies and little children, from the ship to the shore. Anyhow, as we will see, it didn't come to that.

Of course, the *Haganah* wasn't the only one with a plan. Our adversary, the British Navy, had something else in mind. Two or three days after we left the shores of France, a number of British warships appeared on the horizon (five destroyers and one cruiser). They were "escorting" us on our voyage. There was no doubt in our minds that the arrival of the British Navy signaled that they would try to stop us as we approached the shores of Mandatory Palestine. It was also obvious that there was going to be a struggle, albeit between very uneven forces. However, we had no knowledge exactly when the assault would take place. The command, therefore, was issued to immediately fortify the ship. Barbed wire was stretched all around the decks to make it more difficult for the British commandos to take over our ship whenever they decided to attack.

And then we suddenly realized that the assault was about to commence. It was Friday, July 18, 1947, at exactly two and a half hours after midnight. The timing and location of the attack was chosen by the British Navy so as to prevent us from getting too close to shore. They decided to attack us while we were still sailing in the open sea, in international waters. This was, of course, against the Law of the Sea treaty, but it was blatantly clear that, in this case at least, the British navy didn't care much about such formalities. When the British warships started to approach and close in around us, all the youth on our ship were ordered to man pre-arranged "battle stations". The Zionist flag of blue and white was raised high on the mast. Our boat was renamed *Haganah Ship Exodus 1947*, and the passengers and crew burst into enthusiastic singing of *Hatikvah*, the Zionist national anthem.

Radio silence was broken and wireless contact was established between our ship and *Haganah* headquarters on the shore. The various Zionist youth movements were each allocated a certain section of the ship to defend. Our group, *Ken Hatechia*, was ordered to report for the fight in the narrow prow of the ship where we would have a good overview of what was about to happen.

We were provided our "weaponry"—tin cans of various conserves, as well as potatoes. We were both angry and laughing at the same time. Why? Because during our voyage up to that point, we hadn't been provided any potatoes or conserves to eat and we were always hungry. Now suddenly, all these provisions surfaced in order to be thrown at the invading British commandos... as our secret and effective tools of war!

And so the battle began. Out of the six warships, which were escorting us up to that moment, two destroyers took up position adjacent to our ship, one on each side; they were maneuvering to stick to us as close as possible with virtually no gap at all between the destroyers and our ship. The invading ships' decks were higher than ours and the commandos with weaponry in hand, including wooden baseball-type bats, were waiting for the proper moment to jump.

First, they used iron forks to remove the barbed wire at the spots they needed for their attack and then when the alignment of the vehicles was to their liking, they started to jump onto the Exodus. Our men were lined up, having been prepared for something like this. Some of them succeeded in grabbing one or two commandos and throwing them overboard into the water. But there were plenty of British soldiers and those in the water were quickly replaced by fresh assailants. All this time, we were also throwing the tin conserves and the potatoes at the British. It looked like the British warships were losing speed because again and again we found ourselves ahead of them. The attacking destroyers were constantly replaced by the others in reserve. Whenever they caught up with our ship, they banged against its sides again and again. Since ours was made of wood while the destroyers were constructed of steel, it didn't take too long before a huge cavity materialized in the outer panel of our ship.

Beyond, the very young and the old, i.e., the non-fighting passengers, were awaiting the outcome of the battle. The fight went on. In some instances the commandos used their revolvers to shoot at us. Soon enough, three men were dead—two of the *Maapilim* and one of the crew, which was made up of American volunteers and members of other nations, Jews and gentiles alike. The British commandos succeeded in occupying the captain's deck, but there was an alternative place at a lower level from where Ike, our captain, steered and guided the ship.

It soon became apparent because of the large gap in the side of the ship, which was very close to water level, that there was a real danger of our ship sinking. That's when the *Haganah* person in charge of our whole operation decided to surrender. The British took command of our ship and directed it to sail into Haifa harbor.

For us youngsters fifteen, sixteen and seventeen years old, this whole voyage and "fight" was nothing more than an adventure. But three men were killed and a great number wounded. There were also those, especially among the small children, who were close to the gap in our ship and were terrified.

When the skirmish was over, I immediately descended to the lower deck where the smaller children were waiting. We were all tired but still searching for suitable positions from which to better observe Haifa and Mount Carmel, as our ship approached the bay. It was July 18, 1947, 2 o'clock in the afternoon, when we set our eyes on this first sight of *Eretz Yisrael*.

When we arrived at the dock, the wounded on stretchers were lowered first and rushed to hospitals. We considered them quite lucky because they were allowed to remain while it was clear that all the rest of us were going to be deported, we then theorized, to Cyprus.

When our turn came to disembark from the Exodus, three British "liberty" ships were already lined up for us in the harbor—the Empire Rival, the Ocean Vigor and the Renimar Park. We were all together 4,530 *Olim*, so each ship was destined to carry approximately 1,500 people. I, with others, boarded the Empire Rival via a narrow wooden footbridge. Beforehand, however, all of us were disinfected with generous doses of DDT pumped into our hair, clothing and our whole body. This wasn't the last time we were to be disinfected in such a manner and the truth is we didn't mind it very much, even though, as far as I know, DDT is now considered a carcinogen. We all know now about the deep insult felt in the 1950s by the *Olim* from Morocco when subjected to this powder upon their arrival in the already sovereign state of Israel.

There was nothing at all on the British ship to accommodate 1,500 men, women and children. No beds, no cabinets, nothing at all. Among us were young couples, some with babies and small children. They were forced to settle down in the belly of the ship and had to lean and lie on each other. The congestion was terrible. Those were really inhuman conditions, which, as it turned out, all were to suffer for weeks to come. Even then, as just a boy of not even seventeen, I observed the young couples with babies and understood how much more difficult it was for them to endure these circumstances than for us youngsters.

My group was vigilant enough not to settle down in the belly of the ship. We organized a move to the deck where at least there was fresh air. Five of us took hold of a small area that used to be an open-air shower facility of some sort and made it our "home". Later, this place became a sort of command center or at least a hub of activity. Why this developed thus, I don't know. Maybe because of its location on the deck adjacent to the barbed wire fence that separated the deck from the sea. Maybe the place became popular because of the jovial spirit, we, the permanent habitants of this small spot of two and half meters by four, inspired. We called the place "Kirug-Lak" because of its double meaning in Hungarian: "I'll kick you out" and "Home of the Kirug family". Anyhow, the five of us, Sárkány, Kerami, Misi, Irma and I, made this place a base from which to face the adventure awaiting us all.

All three British "Liberty" ships lifted anchor and we headed out to the open sea. We were convinced that our destination was Cyprus, but after a while the experienced among us, who were trying to discern the direction of our ship, noticed something strange. We were sailing to the west and not the northwest, which would have been the logical route to Cyprus. So it seemed that, for some reason, the British had decided to take us to somewhere else and not to Cyprus where they were interning all "illegal" *Olim*.

In order to notify the other ships of this observation, one of our sailors managed to jump into the sea, unobserved by the soldiers guarding us, and started to swim in the direction of one of the other two sister ships.

When the soldiers noticed this man in the water he was already closer to the other ships than to our Empire Rival. Therefore, the British crew of the Ocean Vigor fished him out of the water. When on the deck of this other ship, he told our comrades there the results of our observations, that all three ships were headed due west. I think that this whole "exercise" was unnecessary, because our comrades on board the two other ships had already come to the same conclusion.

Then the two ships converged to be near each other and a cable was shot from Ocean Vigor to Empire Rival. A small cage housing our sailor was placed on the cable and he was returned to us. It was all very exciting for us teenagers on the deck—we loved every second of this adventure in which we unfortunately were only passive participants.

There was very, very little food on board for us. Some biscuits and a little marmalade were distributed from time to time and we were terribly hungry. It was then that I found out that it pays to eat only *kosher* food. Those passengers who ate only kosher were provided with boiled potatoes, which were more nourishing than the marmalade and biscuits. Some of the more "down to earth types" like Peter put ideology aside, declared themselves *kosher* and enjoyed the boiled potatoes.

By the way, there was a story about Peter and his beloved (late) sister Dagi who were constantly looking out for each other. They were born in Vienna to a gentile father and a Jewish mother of Hungarian origin. In 1938, while Germany's annexation of Austria was being enthusiastically celebrated by the Austrians, Dagi, Peter and their mother escaped to Budapest. So, the harsh fate which awaited most of us in Hungary only in 1944 had already started in 1938 for Dagi and Peter. Later, their mother was deported from Kistarcsa, Hungary, to Auschwitz where she perished.

According to the story, Dagi and Peter found themselves together after the war with other Jewish children in *Hashomer Hatzair*'s home in Békéscsaba. The food there was also very scarce. Accordingly, once when they were served soup, right away Peter spat into it to ensure that nobody would take it from him. When I told Peter a couple of years ago about both the kosher potatoes and the spit-soup, he vehemently denied the stories. If they are false, I apologize. I thought them worthwhile mentioning because of the resourcefulness so characteristic of Peter, which trait in him I observed and admired many times in our encounters.

When we became convinced that the ship's goal was not Cyprus, rumors started to make their rounds about our true destination. Finally, we found out that we were being returned to France to the bay of Marseilles. It seems that some sick mind in the British Foreign Ministry had come up with the "bright" idea that since the Exodus's shipload of Jews had started out on its "illegal" journey from France they should be returned to exactly the same spot. This episode only goes to demonstrate that being British, Socialist and a Foreign Minister on top of that, like Mr. Bevin, was no insurance against both stupidity and wickedness. As history evolved, the international upheaval caused by the plight of the Exodus and the nonsensical half-witted reaction of Mr. Bevin to its challenge was one of the reasons why the United Kingdom lost its international mandate in Palestine.

After a few days, we found ourselves, on July 31, 1947, back in the Bay of Marseilles, near the small harbor of Port de Buck. The three Liberty ships lowered anchor. We were back in France.

It didn't take long after our arrival before a number of small vessels, like the ones used by fishermen, popped up along side our ship. In the boat closest to us I noticed a man standing up with a megaphone in his hand pointed in our direction. Then I heard him loud and clear telling us something both in Hebrew and Yiddish, which we immediately understood to be *Haganah* directions as to how we were to conduct ourselves while in anchor there, adjacent to the Port of Sete. We were instructed not to disembark from the ship, not that this order was at all necessary. We understood on our own that the British wanted us returned to the shores of France to the same spot from which we had started out. The British wished thereby to demonstrate their iron will, not to allow "illegal" immigrants to enter Palestine. So it would be Zionist iron will to reach the Land of Israel at all cost, take what it may, against Bevin's iron will to defeat the Zionists in this purpose. The British made it clear again and again that they wanted us to disembark. Thus, our numerous, daily demonstrations started. In English, Hebrew and Yiddish, all the *Olim* on the ships created a commotion, shouting whenever a vessel approached "Open the Gates of Palestine" in English; "*Lo Nered me-Po*" in Hebrew, meaning "We Will Not Disembark", etc.

Because of the very meager food that had been supplied by the British for the voyage back, they agreed to have additional food supplied to us from the shore. Thus, the daily coming and going of various vessels started, bringing food and not only food. A young *Haganah* man, called Giora as his *nom de guerre* (real name, Hana Ishai, who later became one of Ben Gurion's secretaries) joined Gad (real name, Peeri) who had been with us since our July departure from Sete aboard the Exodus. Our conveniently located temporary home, the "Kirug-Lak", often served as a meeting place for the various officials. These *Haganah* men enjoyed demi-god stature as far as my group and most of the *Olim* were concerned. They were wise, they were fearless; they had all the answers.

The days slowly passed and virtually none of the would-be *Olim* left the ship. One of the few exceptions was a twelve-year-old girl in our group, called Kis-Kis-Anya (Little-Little-Mother), who got a severe attack of appendicitis and had to be operated on. Kis-Kis-Anya was one of the Hermann sisters. I know of two additional girls from that family—Nagy-Kis-Anya (Great-Little-Mother) and Kis-Anya (Little-Mother). All three girls were beautiful. To the best of my knowledge, there were also two Hermann brothers, Sanyi and Putyuli.

Kis-Kis-Anya was, of course, taken off the ship because of her illness, accompanied by Rita as her sixteen-year-old guardian. Also during the first days after our arrival in Sete Port, a Hungarian gentile couple who turned out to be British spies were discovered by our leadership and then hurriedly taken off the ship by the British commandant.

As none of the *Olim* volunteered to leave the ships, the British turned to the French authorities for help. The argument was that because the French had allowed the *Haganah* to organize the voyage of the Exodus on French soil and couldn't (or didn't want to) prevent its departure, the French shared responsibility for the fate of the Exodus's passengers and the problem the British were thus facing.

The British even demanded the French authorities use force or allow the British to use force in order to remove us from the three British ships. The French didn't want to use force against us and also denied the British permission to use force. However, the French agreed to offer all the *Olim* asylum, safe passage, even residency in France with permission to live and work there.

To deliver this message, high-ranking French officers were to visit all three ships and address the *Olim*. Our leadership, however, decided that these officers should receive a very special welcome when they addressed the crowd on the Empire Rival. The plan was that when the French officials started to speak, all the *Maapilim* (clandestine immigrants) would burst into singing *Hatikvah* and at the same time the Zionist blue and white flag would be un-furled from the top of the highest mast on the ship.

Yona from our group was a well-known athlete and it was to be his job to carry the flag up the some thirty-meter tall mast. For this purpose, the night before the French delegation was to arrive, Yona, with no one noticing and the flag wrapped around his body, climbed the ladder leading to the top of the mast and hid there in the not too large orifice at the peak of the mast.

The next morning, we all held our breaths waiting for the French to arrive and eagerly anticipating the reaction to our, or more precisely, Yona's stunt. And then the first rumors started to circulate that the French were de-layed, and would only come the next day. It was not only a disappointment but also caused a serious dilemma. It was a very hot day like most of the days we were spending in the bay. The mast was made of steel. For Yona up there it must have felt as if he were enclosed in a hot furnace. He might suffer de-hydration; he might faint and even die in that heat if he stayed all day in his cast iron prison. There was no choice but to get him down, but there was no communication whatsoever with him up there.

So one of our American sailors who was somewhat friendly with the British guards approached them and explained that it appears that one of our boys is missing and maybe, just by accident he had climbed to the top of the mast. The soldiers let our American sailor climb the mast and remove Yona from there, who fortunately was still okay.

The British, who were no dummies, understood that there was some-thing fishy in this young boy "accidentally" climbing the mast. Therefore, after Yona was safely down, they posted a soldier to prevent any such blunder happening again. Yet, we weren't ready to give up on our daring device.

The next morning, while expecting the French delegation at any mo-ment, Yona, with the Zionist blue and white flag again wrapped around his body discreetly moved to stand just beside the ladder leading to the top of the mast. Then, with the French boarding the ship and approaching the captain's bridge, Yona sprinted ahead and rapidly started to climb up the mast while our

American sailor was chatting with the guard. The British guard attempted to pull out his handgun but our sailor put his hand gently on the revolver to deter the soldier, who decided not to shoot. When Yona reached the top, he proudly unfurled our flag. The timing was perfect; everyone was amazed, and most of the *Maapilim* were just as surprised as the British and French. At that very moment the whole crowd burst into singing *Hatikvah*. It was a great, dramatic and memorable moment for all of us. The high-ranking French officers in their dress uniforms still made their speeches about offering French hospitality and residence to all who wanted to stay in France to work and live there. We had the distinct feeling that the French and even the British understood by this time that it was all to no avail and that we were firm and set in our determination to go to the Land of Israel. No one descended from the ships to stay in France and all of the *Maapilim*, especially my group with Yona, our hero, felt wonderful.

Days and even weeks passed. Nothing much changed in our day-to-day lives. It was very warm and food was scarce despite the daily supply by the *Haganah* fishing boats. The French continued in their refusal to remove the *Maapilim* by force and neither would they consent to the British doing so. After all, it was only two years after the war had ended and the world was becoming more and more familiar with the results of the Holocaust in which six million Jews were murdered by the Germans and their accomplices. No wonder there was great commotion in the international community over the behavior of the British government towards the Jewish prisoners on board these three ships. The whole thing started to backfire as far as the United Kingdom was concerned.

Soon enough, the grapevine started to alert us that the three prison ships were going to be moved out of French territory. The rumors proved to be true. On August 19, 1947, after close to a full month in the bay of Marseilles, all three prison ships lifted anchor. We were sailing west. The British government, in its evil stupidity, had decided to take us all the way through Gibraltar and the British Channel, to Hamburg, Germany. It is difficult to decide whether this move was more heinous than foolish, or the other way around.

According to the geopolitical situation after the war, Germany was divided into four allied occupation zones—the Soviet Union, the USA, the United Kingdom and France. Hamburg was part of the British occupation zone and Bevin came to the conclusion that there he would remove us from the ships by force. Can anyone understand this horrible British act as far as morality and world public opinion were concerned? To return Jews to Germany, only two years after the war had ended and the horrible facts of the Holocaust were becoming known worldwide! Dumping Jews in Germany, using force against them on German soil and, as it turned out, imprisoning them behind fences and barbed wire in camps guarded by British soldiers was not only villainy, it was madness, and it strongly backfired against its perpetrators, the British government.

This additional long sea voyage must have been very difficult for those *Olim* who were in the bowels of our prison ships, because of the heat and congestion. When our ship sailed into the Atlantic Ocean and through the Channel, most of the passengers became seasick because of the stormy weather and resultant high waves. This situation, and the fact that most of the *Olim* couldn't eat, was heaven sent for those of us who weren't seasick. For the first time since we had embarked in June aboard the Exodus, we had enough to eat. So we, my group of friends, enjoyed the adventure of sailing into Gibraltar's military harbor for refueling and then the rest of the voyage to Hamburg, as well. We so liked this time spent on the ship, that later in Israel, during the War of Liberation when we enlisted in November 1948, we wanted to become sailors in the Israeli Navy. It didn't work out that way and some of us ended up in the Israeli Air Force, which, as it turned out, was very fortunate for me. However, sailing towards Hamburg on the Empire Rival, I couldn't have foreseen that all this would happen just four short years later.

Jumping forward briefly to 1951, the Air Force sent me to Henlow, England as a 2nd Lieutenant in the Israeli Air Force to study in the Technical University for officers of the Royal Air Force. It was still customary in the RAF for officers to have a personal servant, called a "batman". Therefore, I too was allocated a young British soldier to serve me. He had to press my uniform, make me tea, etc. My servant was a shy young man of maybe eighteen or nineteen and I was twenty one. I was laughing to myself thinking about the jokes fate sometimes plays. Only four years had passed between 1947 and 1951. In 1947, British soldiers were guarding me as their prisoner and in 1951 I was the equal of my fellow British officers and even had one of their own waking me up each morning with his traditional gentle knock on the door and greeting of "Good morning, sir; I've brought you your tea."

BACK IN GERMANY

On September 10, 1947, the Empire Rival was about to enter the harbor of Hamburg. It was now two months since we had first embarked the S.S. Exodus in France. All this time we had spent at sea with only a few minutes at the dock of Haifa. The orders of the *Haganah* for the other two ships, Ocean Vigor and Renimer Park, were to resist by force the British commandos in their efforts to remove the *Olim*. However, for our ship, the Empire Rival, the instructions were not to resist. The reason for this was that Micha Perlman (Gad), one of the *Haganah* fellows on the Empire Rival, had planted a bomb adjacent to one of the outside parapets of the ship to go off after we disembarked. The spot where the bomb was to be placed had been prepared while we were still in the Port of Sete in France. We were often ordered to sing as loud as possible to divert the attention of the soldiers from the noise of the drilling, which went on over many days. So, while on the other two prison ships the *Olim* were clubbed and dragged off by force, we quietly left our ship. I think the reason we were ordered by the *Haganah* to leave peacefully, was to ensure that we would all be off the ship very fast and on the shore when the bomb went off. The bomb, however, never exploded because the British were no dummies either; they probably figured out what was going on and found the bomb before it exploded. It was a very small bomb in any case and would have caused very little damage to the ship.

So there we were on the docks of Hamburg harbor with British soldiers and German police all around. I noticed a high-ranking Scottish officer in a tartan skirt, looking like a general to me, who seemed to be in charge of the operation. We were all herded onto train coaches that were waiting nearby. They were regular passenger cars but with iron grating on the windows and doors. We were still prisoners. The train started to move and I noticed British troops and German police on each side of the rails stationed some ten to twenty meters apart.

The 4,500 *Olim* were taken to two camps near Lübeck. Our smaller camp, only for the passengers of one ship, the Empire Rival, was in Amstau and the rest were taken to a larger camp in Popendorf. Both these facilities were barbed-wire prison camps with watchtowers for the British soldiers who were guarding us.

Arriving in Amstau, each of us was registered by the British. However, we were given instructions by the *Haganah* not to disclose our real names, so each of us decided how he or she wanted to be called. Some took the name Bevin, some were Atlee; I became Rabinovitch.

In the Amstau camp we were soon hungry again. In our desperation to eat well and feel that our bellies were full at least once, we decided to put aside part of our meager rations each day and save it for a special occasion. This grand event arrived when we had plenty of sardines, margarine and bread set aside. From this horde of provisions we prepared sandwiches, a mountain of sandwiches. For the first time, everyone could eat as many sandwiches as he or she wished. We counted the number of sandwiches each of us ate. The winner was a girl, Iren, whose healthy appetite enabled her to pack away some thirty slices of bread with margarine and sardines.

We stayed in Amstau for less than two months. After a while, the guards were removed and we were free to travel to Lübeck and the vicinity. I suppose because our camps were unfit for winter accommodation for so many people, we were moved on October 10, 1947 to another camp in Sengwarden near Wilhelmshaven, even more to the north than Lubeck. This was a former German Navy base, an ultramodern facility by the standards of those days. For instance, the fact that the various halls and rooms were connected with a vacuum-operated letter delivery system, made a great impression on every one of us. One had to place his letter in a small container, which exactly fitted into the tubing, and the vacuum sucked the container with the letter in its belly to its destination.

We stayed in Sengwarden for a little less than three months. The boys decided to learn to drive. So we located a driving school and started to take lessons from a middle-aged German instructor who owned a small Volkswagen. German money, the Reichsmark, was still in circulation at the time, but had no real purchasing power; therefore, cocoa served as our means of payment for the driving lessons. After several lessons on the small Volkswagen and just before our driving tests, we came to the conclusion that this was not *it*. It just was *not it*. After all, we were on our way to *Eretz Yisrael* to become *Chalutzim* (pioneers), and it wouldn't do to be able to drive only such a small car. We were going to be workers there, proletariat, not bourgeois. We demanded that our instructor get us a large truck, a semi-trailer for our lessons. "No problem," he said. "It's just a matter of some additional cocoa." So we brought him more cocoa and a huge semi-trailer materialized out of nowhere. There was not much time left before the tests, which were already scheduled, so I got to sit in the cabin only once, with the huge steering wheel in my hands, and drove the truck only for a few hundred meters.

The day of the driver's license test arrived. We all settled into the trailer itself waiting for our turn to be tested, but not before we discreetly handed over to our instructor the agreed portion of cocoa, for him and the tester. Each candidate for the driver's license was called in turn to the front of the trailer. Both the tester and our instructor were already sitting in the right-hand side of the cabin.

In addition to our group in the trailer, there were young German men as well, each of them very nervous because of the importance of the occasion. For them, it was a serious test of driving aptitude. We, however, were calm. Our licenses were well protected by the cocoa portion intended for the tester, which was already in the safe hands of our instructor. After a while, my turn to be tested arrived. I moved to the cabin and settled into the driver's seat. This was only the second, and last, time in my life that I was in a semi-trailer's driver's seat. This huge trailer was parked off the main road, adjacent to a house with a concrete fence. "Please start to drive, Mr. Sichermann," our instructor commanded. I put the lever in gear but instead of the first gear to start moving ahead, I put the lever into reverse by mistake and pushed the gas pedal as hard as I could. The cabin, plus the trailer attached to it, gave a jolt... backwards. After all, the gear was in reverse. The trailer hit the concrete fence behind us with a loud crashing sound and the engine stalled. "Thank you, Mr. Sichermann," the tester said, "you have passed the test." He wasn't joking. An hour or so later, when we drove back to the tester's office, I was handed my driver's license issued in Jever, Germany, with my name and picture, granting me a license in the year 1947 to drive a semi-trailer in Germany. I still keep that license and guard it with great pride! It is always good for a laugh when I recount this story among those friends who haven't heard it yet. Oh, the great magic and various wonders performed by cocoa (and cigarettes, chocolate, etc.) in post-war Germany!

There is another funny story from Sengwarden that I have to relay, which has to do with Misi. I mentioned before that all of us took on false names to confuse the enemy, i.e. the British. I was "Rabinovitch" and so was Misi. At the time, we were best friends so we shared the same name.

One afternoon in Sengwarden, Misi and I, with others as well, were in one of the larger halls when the Scottish camp commander entered. "I am looking for Misi Friedmann," he said. "There is no such person here," answered Misi himself. "Are you sure?" asked the Scot. "Are you absolutely sure?" he asked again. "His parents want him to be returned home to Hungary." "No, we don't know anyone called Friedmann Misi," we all replied. The camp commander looked unconvinced but had no choice and after a while left the room. The background of this story is that Misi's father, Ede Friedmann, the same person who on January 1, 1946 accompanied us to the Southern Railroad station in Buda, having heard from the media about the harsh fate of the passengers on the Exodus, decided to "save" his son from the Zionists. He went to the British Embassy in Budapest to complain about the Zionists who had "abducted" his only son. Misi had a sister, Ági, but no brother. Misi's father was even interviewed by the BBC, where he repeated his story about the "abduction" of Misi by the Zionist Movement.

This is not the end of the Friedmann story. In 1956, after the Hungarian Revolution, he and his wife, Misi's mother, escaped from Hungary. They traveled to England, to some relatives living there. It wasn't long though before they decided that England was not the place for them and made *Aliya* to Israel. They became new immigrants with all the rights a new immigrant was entitled to upon arrival in Israel. They settled down but didn't feel at home here either. So, later, they returned to Hungary where Ági, their daughter was still living. However, even this wasn't the end of their wanderings. They subsequently shuttled quite a number of times between Israel and Hungary. Finally, the mother passed away in Israel and the father, years later, passed away in Hungary where, at the time, he was living with Ági.

On November 29, 1947, we heard on the radio in Sengwarden, as did Jews all over the world, to the historic decision taken by the United Nation's General Assembly to create an independent state for the Jewish people in part of Mandatory Palestine. To be frank, for me at least, this great and historic development came as a total surprise because I was under the impression that all we were fighting for was *Aliya Hofshit*, or free immigration, for all the Jews who wanted to live in *Eretz Yisrael*. Maybe this delusion was caused by the political attitude of *Hashomer Hatzair*, which at the time was still in the mindset of a bi-national state, shared by Jews and Arabs. Maybe the fault was in me personally by not fully understanding the political realties and comprehending the goals of the Jewish Agency leadership. Anyhow, we also celebrated when the results of the voting were announced.

At the time, we didn't realize yet what an important role our ship, the S.S. Exodus, and all of us *Maapilim* played in creating a very positive world opinion in favor of Jewish independence. The general opinion among us was that the Arabs wouldn't accept the partition of the Land of Israel and would start to fight against it. It was also estimated by the more knowledgable that if there was going to be a fight with the local Palestinian Arabs only, our side would have the upper hand.

There were grave doubts, however, whether the *Yishuv* (the Jewish population in the country) could overcome the regular armies of the Arab states like Egypt, Transjordan, Syria, etc., should they choose to intervene.

GOING HOME

On February 11, 1948 we left Sengwarden on our way again to *Eretz Yisrael*. The *Haganah* had decided that all the *Maapilim* of the Exodus should make it into Mandatory Palestine by hook or by crook. There were three categories of *Aliya* at the time: *Aliya Alef* or legal *Aliya*, *Aliya Bet* or clandestine *Aliya* as in the Exodus, and *Aliya Daled* with forged or false papers. (Why there wasn't an *Aliya Gimel*, I will never know.) So since *Aliya Bet* failed us, we were to try *Aliya Daled*, i.e., sneak into Palestine with false papers.

Our first stop after Sengwarden was the camp at Bergen-Belsen, not the former concentration camp, which was burned down by the British as a health precaution, but in the former quarters of the SS. The place was run by the Jewish Agency and served as a temporary breather for Jews on their way to *Eretz Yisrael*. What struck me as bizarre was the large number of pianos lined up in the corridors waiting to be crated and shipped. Why pianos, for what purpose, who were the owners, to be shipped where? Only God knows. It was very queer. We were idealists fighting for our right to live in our own land and, at the same time, someone else was worrying about pianos.

We stayed in Bergen Belsen for only a very short time and then we were off to Southern France, arriving in Marseilles sometime in March 1948. After a couple of days there, I received a letter from my Aunt Jolan in Paris. As I later found out, my other aunt, Margit, who lived in Wilkes-Barre, Pennsylvania, had inquired after the war, via the American Embassy in Budapest, whether anyone of her family had survived. Margit was my father's older sister. She was born in 1897. My father was born on August 30, 1900. Thus Margit found out that I was alive. Margit was in contact with Jolan, her sister-in-law, and notified her about her discovery. Margit's late brother, Miksa (born 1878), was the oldest of the Sichermann siblings. Jolan started to search for me via the Joint and the UNRRA and located me in Marseilles just as I arrived there.

I answered Jolan's letter and she sent me money for a ticket from Marseilles to Paris. So I took the train and traveled to Paris. I have already recounted how I missed Jolan and the others at the railroad station and in consequence encountered Jenő before I met any of the other members of my family. I stayed in Paris a week or so, was very impressed and had a wonderful time. But herein lies a tale related to my subsequent *Aliya*.

Aunt Jolan and Jenő lived in a small apartment on 15 Rue de la Clef, not far from a metro station. The premises do not exist anymore, it was dismantled in the 1970s and new, modern apartment buildings were erected on the site. In the spring of 1948 the old building was still there. It was a very ancient house. There was no W.C. inside the apartment. In between two floors there was an old fashioned toilet, reminding me of the one in the courtyard on Szarvas Street in Nyiregyháza. The toilet was for the use of the tenants living on the floors, above and below.

Jenő had been a blacksmith originally in Transylvania and also in his early days in Paris before the war. After the war he became a tailor. He worked at home in their apartment, which was very small, but always full with family and friends. The intimate Sichermann-Rubinstein family consisted of Jolan (born on January 15, 1894), Jenő (born 1896) and Jolan's son, my cousin Laci (born 1916). Laci was newly wed to Edit (born in Hamburg, on December 26, 1924).

Then there was Böske, Jolan's oldest daughter, who was, of course, also my cousin. Böske was divorced from Józsi who was a hairdresser, as was Böske. They had a son, Zsozso, who was three years younger than I. In 1936, Bözsi and Zsozso visited us in Nyiregyháza. Zsozso was three years old at the time and was a spoilt, very undisciplined child. Zsozso was an only child, just like me. An only child is usually too pampered and therefore tends to be spoiled. I know it from my own personal experience.

Anyhow, during their visit in 1936, Böske and Zsozso stayed with us on Szarvas Street, where we had a wooden gate with a very large iron key to open and close the lock. One morning, Zsozso took hold of this key and, standing very close to me, smashed it on my head with all his force. No wonder everyone in our household, including me, was very happy when we finally accompanied Böske and Zsozso to the train station on their way back to Paris.

Böske, who was divorced from Józsi, unrealistically hoped all her life that one day she would regain her husband who had remarried another woman, but she never did, of course. Zsozso, as a grown-up, also became a hairdresser. He married an African beauty queen whom he met serving in a French overseas department of the French Army in Martinique. They have three sons and later lived and worked in Strasbourg. Laci and Edit kept me updated about him and his family, but I never met either Zsozso or his family again, besides the encounter with him in 1936. Unfortunately, I never met Jolan's youngest daughter, Margit (born 1920). She was deported in 1942 and perished.

Laci was drafted into the French Army when the war broke out and with the capitulation was incarcerated by the Germans as a prisoner of war. He somehow escaped and found his way to the "unoccupied" zone of France. Later, he joined the French Underground and fought the Germans and their French collaborators until the Liberation in 1944. In 1947, Laci and Edit married. Edit was, and still is, a very sweet and warm woman. Laci and Edit had a harmonious married life together until May 2001, when Laci silently passed away at the age of 85 sitting in his armchair at their home in Maison Alfort on the outskirts of Paris. They have a daughter, Sylvia, who lives with her mother and is unmarried.

In 1948, during my first visit to Paris, Edit showed me around the city. The city at the time was very quiet, with no tourists to be seen anywhere, contrary to the Paris of today.

Jenő has three children from his first marriage. His first wife was also deported during the war and perished in Auschwitz. Their older daughter, Claire, lives in Israel and has no children. Another daughter and a son live in France. In the 1960s and 1970s, I visited Jolan-Jenő and Edit-Laci many times in Paris and both couples have also visited us quite a few times in Israel.

In 1948, however, during my first visit there, the whole family tried to convince me to stay with them in Paris. I remember one of their arguments: "Why go to Palestine? Stay here in France with us and become a Communist, just like we are." In 1990, Edit and Laci visited and stayed with us in our home in Bayside, New York. I tried to remind Laci about this business of "... Communist, just like us..." but he denied that they were ever Communists. He said that I might have confused the facts. He mentioned that they had a distant relative who *was* a Communist and maybe this person was the one who expressed himself in such a manner. Well, I don't know. Maybe Laci was right. I know that sometimes human memory can be misleading. The only question concerning this particular issue is whose memory is playing tricks, Laci's or mine?

Over the years, Laci and I and our families met many times in France, in Israel and in New York. We talked a lot about politics. In the beginning, Laci was neutral as to the Israeli situation but he became more and more involved, at least as far as his feelings went. He became very strongly pro-Israel; however, he spotted the dangers of Jewish religious fanaticism right after the Six Day War in 1967. I remember him saying to me once at that time that he didn't like the religious fervor as demonstrated by the too ardent praying at the Wailing or Western Wall. I hadn't noticed this phenomenon in such a critical way before Laci opened my eyes to it, and he was right in foreseeing the events which followed later. These were the first signs of the "Messiah madness", which in the years thereafter took hold of such large sectors among Orthodox Jews in our country.

Laci was also a French patriot. As such, he didn't like the Americans very much. Still, when Edit and Laci stayed with us in New York, he confessed how impressed he was with what he observed as the high morale of the American working person and his devotion to his workplace. He had a somewhat contradictory notion of French antisemitism. On the one hand, he fervently denied the existence of it in France, while, on the other hand, he changed his last name from the Jewish-sounding Sichermann to the typical French name, Pradel. He also asked us not to speak Hungarian in the elevator of the high rise where he lived, "because speaking Hungarian indicates that one is an immigrant, which in the French mind is an indication of being Jewish."

Well, as I have already mentioned, during my stay in Paris in the spring of 1948, all of my relatives tried to convince me not to return to Marseilles but to stay with them. I refused and insisted that I had a responsibility to my *Hashomer Hatzair* group in Marseilles, especially the children in my care. I clearly remembered the trauma caused to all of us by the sudden disappearance of Ervin Birnbaum when he left Amstau to return to his parents in Kosice, Slovakia. By the way, when I eventually returned to Marseilles I found that some of my group there were convinced that I wouldn't come back and even started to discuss how to divide up my meager belongings, which I had left behind.

I have often asked myself later on for the real reason of my return to Marseilles. To be quite frank, by that time in March 1948, I wasn't too enthusiastic anymore about traveling to Mandatory Palestine. As a result of the wanderings of the previous two and a half years in Germany, France, at sea, etc., most of us were fed up. In addition, the war was already raging there. The Arabs of Mandatory Palestine had started rioting and attacking Jews immediately after the UN Resolution of November 29, 1947. I wasn't in the mood to be part of a new war less than three years after the Second World War. Now, when I write these notes after near endless hostilities with the Palestinian Arabs, and five or six proper wars with our various Arab neighbors, my qualms from March 1948 are very vivid indeed.

It is true that I personally gained a lot by coming to Israel in April 1948. First of all, it was clear, after a somewhat difficult start, that I was at home at last, in my own country. I was, and still am, a first-class citizen in all respects. Settling in Israel, one might say, even pampered me. In 1951, as already mentioned, I was chosen to study in England for thirteen months at the Technical College for officers of the Royal Air Force. In 1956, I was sent to Haifa for four years to the Technion (Israel Institute of Technology), where I obtained my engineering degree. I have had an excellent professional career, which I am proud of, including a number of very challenging and interesting jobs and responsibilities. Of course, my career in the Air Force and later in Israel Aircraft Industries, were both the result of my having first joined the Air Force's School of Mechanics in 1948.

We have established a lovely family consisting of two daughters and now also six grandchildren. So, from my own selfish point of view, everything went my way. My query and question marks relate to the future of my offspring here in Israel. The animosity of the Arab world around us, the shortsightedness of our politicians and the centrifugal social forces constantly threatening to break up our less and less democratic society, frightens me mostly as it affects the future of the young generation.

Still, I have to try to answer the question I have often posed to myself about the real reason for having decided then, in 1948, not to remain in Paris with my relatives. Maybe my decision was influenced by the fact that Jolan's apartment was so small. It had only two rooms—a bedroom for Jolan and Jenő, which also served as his workroom where he pressed the trousers and other garments he was working on. The second room was the living room used for all other purposes including the folding bed I slept on. There was a small kitchen, but I don't remember any bathroom and, as I have mentioned before, the toilet was in the corridor between the floors.

Could I have stayed in Paris, given my relatives' difficult economic circumstances? Maybe yes; maybe no; I really don't know. As I said, I wasn't very eager anymore to go to *Eretz Yisrael*. However, knowing myself as I am, it is quite possible that had I chosen to stay in Paris and not return to my responsibilities and my comrades in Marseilles, I would have suffered pangs of a bad conscience all my life. Anyhow, for whatever reasons, I decided to return to Marseilles and rejoin my group on our journey to still-Mandatory Palestine.

My relatives asked me what I wished for as a parting present. Since I was about to start shaving and wasn't enthusiastic about using a razor and sheath like my friend Misi, I asked for an electric shaver. This request was met with raised eyebrows. Electric shavers were considered a luxury in 1948 and it was really stupid to ask for one. But I got my Philips electric shaver with one shaving head, which I haven't used much, as it wasn't very effective in giving me a close shave. Still, I was silently laughing to myself when, in the 1980s and 1990s, Laci proudly displayed for me his large collection of all sorts of electric shavers. By then, he only shaved electrically.

I took the train, returned to Marseilles and a couple of days later we were scheduled to board the ship, Kedma, for our voyage to Haifa. Not, however, before I clashed with the Jewish Agency person in charge of the facility where we resided during our stay in Marseilles.

There still wasn't enough food and the children were hungry all the time. When we complained about this, we were told that these were all the rations allocated and nothing could be done about it. Then came the farewell party and dinner, which was a lavish occasion with so much food served that we couldn't eat it all. So I, as the self-appointed ringleader, confronted the person in charge and expressed our dissatisfaction with his policy of having let the children go hungry all that time in order to create this feast at the end. Why I thus complained is hard to say. Frankly, now it seems to me that I behaved quite silly at the time, but I do have this weakness of convincing myself of some sort of "injustice", which I have to confront, and then running amok!

When boarding the Kedma the next day, this Jewish Agency guy was sitting on the ship's deck recording the names and particulars of each passenger. When it was my turn to come to his desk, he angrily addressed me, "I have made a report about you to the authorities in Haifa. When you get there they will treat you accordingly." This was even more stupid of him than my behavior of the night before was childish. I laughed to myself. This threat coming from him was so obviously hollow nonsense. Israel was at war. The last concern of the people there was the "insult" I hurled against this "representative of Jewish independence-to-come".

So after several days of a very pleasant and comfortable voyage, very different from our previous experience at sea, we arrived in Haifa. I was traveling with a false certificate of immigration issued by the authorities of the British Mandate in Palestine. My name, according to this paper, was Tibor Goldmann born in Győr, Hungary, in the year 1927—I was supposedly three years older than I really was. So, I was a little concerned when on our arrival in Haifa the British Immigration Officer examined my papers and compared my picture that carefully replaced the original one of Tibor, whom, of course, I had never met, neither before nor after. However, all went well and we were free to descend from the ship. It was just at the time when the battle for Haifa between Jews and Arabs was raging. We mounted the "armored" cars waiting for us and traveled through the lower city adjacent to the port, originally in the Arab parts of Haifa. We heard shooting and observed traces of fighting through the narrow shutters of the vehicle, but we were not shot at. We were quite lucky in this because those armored cars were not much more than some metal plates mounted above and around an old truck.

We safely passed the danger zone and arrived at the "checkpost" on the outskirts of Haifa. There we descended from the armored vehicles and climbed into a small old-fashioned bus that was waiting for us. The bus then immediately started on its way, following a narrow asphalt road, which served as the main thoroughfare between the checkpost and the small towns located to the north of the Haifa bay. After a journey of some twenty minutes we arrived at our first residence in *Eretz Yisrael*, the *Olim* camp in Kiryat Yam.

Asher, Vice President of Israel Aircraft Industries, with, among others, Prime Minister Menachem Begin and Defense Minister Ezer Weizman, circa 1976

Asher's family today

It was Sunday, April 18, 1948.
In September, I would turn eighteen.
The third phase of my life had just ended.
The fourth, Israel, was beginning!
At last, I was
HOME

CHAPTER 5

FRIENDS

Friends from Nyiregyháza

Gruenspan Józsi, Poper Ede, Gruenfeld Tibi, Weishaus Tomi, Altmann Gyuri, Klein Tigi, Moskovits Gabi, Renyi Gyuri, Kuhn Laci, Breier Gyuri (Boengi), Taub Ernő, Leitner Imre, Ganzfried Gyuri, Klein Pista, Vermes Robi, Schwartz Zoli, Lipkovits Pista, the Balázs brothers, Jancsi and his older brother, Teitelbaum Evi, and Lila.

Tomi Weishaus was an only son. His mother survived deportation but both Tomi and his father perished. Tomi was a little chubby, maybe even a fat boy, with a sharp wit and a wonderful sense of humor. We used to fool around a lot. His father was a baker and they lived on Vay Adam Street. Tomi used to bring buttered crisp rolls with salami to school and when in a good mood he agreed to share one with me. I just loved those fresh rolls. He was the first to have a fountain pen. It was a German design, called a "Tintenkuli". In those days, in the thirties and early forties, we still used regular pens and ink pots.

Gyuri Altmann was also an only son. His mother returned from the concentration camp but Gyuri and his father perished. Gyuri's parents owned a haberdashery adjacent to the central market place and to the *Megyehaz* (the Central Headquarters of the District Government). Because they had a store with all those wonderful buttons, Gyuri had a lot of them at his disposal at home. When I went to visit him—they lived in a little alcove-type apartment near their store—we usually played soccer with the buttons; the large ones were the players, the largest, the goal keeper and the smallest, the ball.

Joska Gruenspan was a delicate boy. He was good-looking but a little shy. They lived in a small apartment in a courtyard also on Vay Adam Street. Besides Tomi and Joska, as I mentioned above, Pista Klein, as well as Gabi Moskovits, lived on that same street. I never heard anything about Joska Gruenspan or his family after the war. I am afraid they all may have perished.

The parents of Gabi Moskovits had a small store, across from their apartment and adjacent to the Urania Cinema. They sold agricultural machinery. Gabi had two older brothers. The rumor after the war was that the oldest brother, called I think, Gyuri, survived because of some peculiar good fortune. Before the German occupation, he was arrested by the police for some reason or other and forgotten about when the Jews were deported to Auschwitz. Thus, he was "safely" tucked away in prison during the whole period of deportation. Gabi was a lively, talented boy who didn't put too much effort into learning but was gifted in music.

Together with Pista Lipkovits and others, we used to play *Capitaly* (a Monopoly variant), which was *the* hit game among us at the time. Gabi was especially dedicated to the game and wanted to make a lot of "money" and he loved to build "houses and hotels". To make the game more challenging he even used colored paper to prepare additional millions in currency in order to be able to buy more lots and install buildings, much more than originally planned by the folks who had designed the game. It's funny how memory works—I still remember my astonishment at Gabi one day. While we were playing in the hallway of their apartment, Gabi's mother was pickling tomatoes for the winter. Gabi was eating the raw vegetable, one tomato after the other. In Hungary in those days, we usually ate raw green pepper and green onions and radish but never raw tomatoes.

In the house of Tigi Klein we used to play table tennis. Tigi was very good. I wasn't too bad, but couldn't get above a certain level of achievement. This is very characteristic of me. Most things I did in life, I was quite good at, but I did not really excel in anything. I gave sort of a 70% to 85% performance—not below, not above, never 95%.

Gyuri Renyi didn't survive but his pretty, gifted older sister, Erzsi, did. Gyuri was a year older than me. I remember him from my first day in first grade. We, the new kids in first grade, were being led into our classroom when the boys from second grade stormed out of their classroom. Together with his classmates there he was, Gyuri Renyi, shouting at us *pocosok, pocosok*, which translates as "fresh meat, fresh meat". I think that the reason I especially remember him from that occasion is due to fact that I noticed his larger than average head tilted slightly to the right. Renyi Gyuri was a gifted boy, the little boy of Dr. Renyi who was an attorney. After the war their house, well-located in the center of town, was used by the local Jewish relief organizations.

Ernő Taub was a religious boy. We attended together the four grades of the Jewish elementary school. There was a time when we lived in the same neighborhood and often walked home together. Ernő had a very good friend, Leitner or Letra as we called him. I had great respect for Ernő, especially after I witnessed once the way he had beaten up an older gentile boy who said something nasty to him. Ernő beat this boy like hell. I was proud of him; it was very rare for a Jewish kid to beat up a gentile boy. Usually, it was the other way around. Both Taub and Leitner survived deportation and, as I write these notes they are neighbors and work together in a *Moshav*, a small farm settlement, near Ashdod.

I sometimes try to imagine what would have become of my friends had they all survived. Most of those who survived had a good life with nice careers. Emil Hahn is now Dr. Hahn, a professor at the Technical University of Budapest. Robi Vermes is a professor of mathematics in Montreal. Pista Lipkovits raised a large and wonderful family of four children and numerous grandchildren and is a founding member of his Kibbutz, Gaaton, in Upper Galilee. Laci Kuhn became a well-known painter in Israel; Boengi did his doctorate in metallurgy, and before retiring, was a professor at the Technion.

Friends from Aliya to Eretz Yisrael

The boys were: Jonas (Yona), Misi, Dov (his original Hebrew name was Tov, but the guys didn't like it so they renamed him Dov), Kuka (because he was small and looked like one of the dwarfs in Snow White), Rafi, Yussuf, Ali,

David and Hosszu (because someone believed that he was too tall) and Asher or Ashi. i.e., myself.

The girls were: Sárkány (because once she shouted at the other girls who didn't clean up the tent), Hava, Tamar and Yardena.

Later on in our long journey to *Eretz Yisrael* some of the above boys "dated" some of the above girls and thus boy-girl friendships flourished. Misi and Hava, Rafi and Tamar, Ashi and Sárkány were such couples.

Jonas, or Yona Mandel, came from the ninth district in Budapest. Not too many Jews lived there. Roughly speaking, the ninth was a working class district. Jonas's father also perished in the war. He was a professional truck driver, also a very non-Jewish occupation. Jonas studied at an industrial high school. He was among the few, including Misi, who knew what they wanted to do when they grew up. Jonas wanted to become an industrial expert and he did. First, he was a first-class aviation mechanic in Israel and later in California; then he switched professions and became a plumber working in building construction, in which he also excelled, even erecting several condominiums through his own business. Jonas now lives in California, married to Ági and has two daughters and a number of grandchildren.

Misi, or Eli Friedmann-Shalev, who unfortunately passed away some years ago, came from the seventh district, the most Jewish district in Budapest. His whole family, parents and only sister, survived the war. Misi attended the same industrial high school as Jonas. Misi, too, knew early in his life that he wanted to work in industry. He also became a very successful aircraft mechanic and despite not having a university education he was more knowledgeable than many highly educated persons I have met in my career in aviation. No wonder Jonas and Misi, with their similar ambitions and talent, were rivals for most of the years we were all together.

I owe to both Jonas and Misi the fact that I became a graduate engineer despite my natural tendencies, which were more in the direction of the humanities. They were firm in their plans to go into industry and when we were eighteen years old, convinced me to go along with them. Luckily, I had enough sense that at that fateful junction of our lives, in November 1948, I joined them to become an aircraft mechanic in the Israeli Air Force. My career was an outcome of that one decision. Misi was married twice and has two children as well as grandchildren.

Dov Koffler (now Dov Laor) was a quiet, very well-behaved boy. He came from a family of three children. His brother was the oldest of three and his sister was second. Luckily, the whole Koffler family survived the war. However, Dov's brother, who became a high-ranking officer in Communist Hungary, died very young. His sister also passed away, although much later. Dov's parents didn't consent to his going on *Aliya*. Despite their resistance, Dov decided to run away, and so he did. Such was the power of post-war Zionism for the young in Hungary that the pride of being in the Movement and the fraternity of friends coupled with the desire to leave together for the "Promised Land" were forces which couldn't be defeated.

Dov also became an aircraft mechanic in Israel but what he really likes to do is to cook. In addition, Dov was always a "ladies' man". The girls chased him instead of him chasing them, but because everybody liked Dov, nobody was jealous of him. Well, maybe just a little! He also married twice and has four children and a number of grandchildren. Dov is my good friend. He reminds me a little of Pista Klein, who had he lived, I guess, would also have turned out to be a ladies' man.

Kuka was a very thin but strong, short guy. Because of his height, somebody must have thought that he resembled one of the dwarfs in the story of Snow White, and therefore was given this name. Because of his short height, I think, he was also very shy. Despite this, Kuka was immediately drafted when he stepped off the ship, which brought him to *Eretz Yisrael* in the spring of 1948. Thus in the War of Independence, Kuka proudly served as a fighter in one of the better units of the Israeli Army.

Rafi (Stern) had one brother, Berci, who, with Rafi and their mother, survived the war. The father perished in the Holocaust. Berci, for a short while, lived and worked in the United States and then returned to Israel. Unfortunately, he fell ill and passed away while still a quite young man. He is survived by his wife and two children. Rafi was the first among all our friends to marry. He and Shula, his wife, have three children, numerous grandchildren and a great-grandchild, as well. As a youngster, Rafi was gifted in drawing but later gave it up almost completely. He was a very diligent, kind-hearted man and fits the type of person best defined by the maxim, "a friend in need is a friend indeed".

Yussuf-Peter Solt, his mother and younger brother all survived the war. The father, however, perished. Yussuf's younger brother remained with his mother in Hungary and made a remarkable career. He became the Chief Justice of Hungary.

Ali or Moshe Feldmann passed away a number of years ago. I liked Ali very much. For a number of years we were good friends. Ali had two sisters and a brother. Their mother and the four children survived the war but the father perished. His younger sister, Dezi, accompanied Ali to the train on that important winter morning in 1946. Someone gave her a little wine to celebrate the occasion of our departure and she became a little tipsy. She was a girl full of life and later immigrated to Australia, where she passed away some years ago. Tovi-Teri, Ali's older sister, lives in Israel. With remarkable will and determination and without any help from the outside world, she finished her long and tedious studies at the Hebrew University of Jerusalem to eventually become a professor of sciences there. Ali's younger brother lives in Hungary and is a civil engineer. Ali is survived by a daughter and two grandchildren.

I lost sight of David in Israel. He married in Petah Tikva and worked in the jewel-cutting business of his wife's family.

Hosszu didn't make much impact on our group during the three years that we were together. He didn't speak much, didn't actively participate in our activities. In 1948, when we were already in Israel, he "discovered" that he was a Communist at heart and returned to Hungary. We never heard anything from him directly after that but there were some rumors that upon his arrival there he was sent to a camp for enemies of the regime to be "re-educated".

Sárkány, or Tova, Rózsika Benedek and I married in Israel in May 1953. Unfortunately, after a cruel but heroic struggle for eleven years against cancer, she passed away in 1994. We have two beautiful daughters, Michal and Merav, and six lovely grandchildren: one girl, Noah, and five boys—Tom, Edan, Omri, Yotam and Uri. Tom, Edan and Omri are Michal and Yariv's and Yotam, Noah and Uri are Merav and Rami's children.

Sárkány was one of the girls who left Hungary for *Eretz Yisrael* without her mother's permission. Her father was murdered in the war by the Hungarian Army while serving in one of their military forced-labor units. Her mother Erzsébet, brother Tomi (Avri, or Benoe) and Sárkány survived. At the time that Sárkány asked her mother's permission to make *Aliya*, Tomi, eighteen months younger, was already on his way through Germany with his group of comrades. Erzsébet agreed to Tomi's departure because without a father it was difficult to discipline him. But she didn't want Sárkány to leave as well. However, the force of attraction exerted by the ideas of Zionism and the wish to be with her comrades was irresistible. Sárkány made up a story to her mother about going for a week to a winter camp in the mountains of Buda, but instead joined us on the train for Vienna, Austria. By chance, I saw Sárkány a couple of days before our departure, January 1, 1946, on one of the streets of Budapest dragging herself along with a huge white knapsack on her back, going, as I later found out, to a friend's home to spend a night or two there before our journey.

Asher and his late wife, Sárkány (Tova), 1953

Unfortunately, Tomi (Avri) passed away several years ago. He is survived by his son, Amir, and their daughter, Orit, who both have three children. Erzsébet, or Elisheva in Hebrew, passed away at the age of ninety five and has four grandchildren and twelve great-grandchildren. Tamar, lovely, beautiful Tamar, was killed in a car accident in Israel in 1950. A jeep driven by Dov overturned in the fields of Kibbutz Negba, wounding some and killing Tamar on the spot. Yardena now lives in Omer, a nice neighborhood in the vicinity of Beer Sheva, in the south of Israel. She is married and has a nice family.

Generation after generation is bound up with our gathering on January 1, 1946 at the train station in Budapest on our way home to *Eretz Yisrael*.